LOVE,
LUCY

LOVE, LUCY

Lucille Ball

with *Betty Hannah Hoffman*

Foreword by Lucie Arnaz

G. P. PUTNAM'S SONS
New York

G. P. Putnam's Sons
Publishers Since 1838
200 Madison Avenue
New York, NY 10016

Library of Congress Cataloging-in-Publication Data
Ball, Lucille, date.
Love, Lucy / Lucille Ball :
foreword by Lucie Arnaz.
p.   cm.
ISBN 0-399-14205-3 (acid-free paper)
1. Ball, Lucille, 1911–1989.   2. Entertainers—
United States—Biography.   I. Title.
PN2287.B16A3   1996
791.45'028'092—dc20
[B]   96-20751   CIP

Printed in the United States of America
10 9 8 7 6 5 4 3 2 1

This book is printed on acid-free paper. ∞

Book design by Deborah Kerner

Foreword

One of my mother's favorite things to do, when a small group of people were involved in some ordinary conversation, was to wait until one of them left the room and as soon as she returned, blurt out, convincingly, "Here she is now! Why don'tcha tell her to her face?!!" This was always followed by frozen silence, and then she'd howl (with that depth-of-the-sea laugh she had) to see the look on the poor soul's face, who for one horrible moment thought someone had been saying terrible things about her while she was gone.

I'm not sure why, but I keep thinking about that now as I sit down to introduce you to this treasure.

LUCILLE BALL

♥

I lost my father at five minutes after midnight on December 2, 1986, and my mother at dawn, on April 26, 1989. For my brother, Desi, and me, it has been a difficult and complicated mourning period.

Normally, I would think, when an adult child loses her first parent, there's a parent's spouse there to take over; to handle the technical decisions, to bury and bequeath. My parents were divorced in the late fifties and both were married to others for more than twenty years. My father's wife, Edie, died of cancer the year before he did, so we were his only heirs. And after my mother's death, her husband of twenty-seven years, and our stepfather, Gary Morton, learned from her executors that he had been very lovingly and carefully provided for, but that she had placed Desi and me in charge of her estate.

For *any* children, tending to an estate is an unwelcome and painful process, no matter when the loss comes. Being the one responsible for making all the important "final" decisions can be a great burden and an instant maturing process all at the same time.

The organizing alone is overwhelming . . . from ridiculous details like who gets the gravy boat to selling the house, to *where* are you going to put all the stuff you simply aren't ready to part with, to choosing what kind of service you think your parent would want (without ever having talked with her about it).

Well, we did it, not once, but twice, within three years, *and* these were not ordinary parents. An old hat box with a rusted zipper, filled with graying white gloves, without fingertips, which you'd assume was "toss it" material, hardly worthy of the thrift-shop pile, becomes a priceless museum piece when you realize that those gloves were worn by the "Professor" character my mother immortalized on the *I Love Lucy* show. Every gown or pocketbook, every seemingly trivial possession that happened to be engraved, became instant "memorabilia." We had to think twice before putting it anywhere.

My brother, Desi, and I debated the importance of preserving those things, and (considering the frame of mind we were in at the time) the process often turned into *hours* of discussions about human destiny and the twisted priorities of would-be scavengers, often either reducing us both to tears of longing and numbness, or giving way to hysterical fantasies of building life-size sculptures of Vitameatavegamin with all the leftover henna rinse. (After watching what happened to the Jacqueline Kennedy Onassis estate, I wish we had sold it by the *ounce* and donated the proceeds to AIDS research!)

Oddly, in some ways, after all these years, life goes on as if they were still here; simply off somewhere, on location perhaps, and unable to get to a phone. If you go by the daily requests for their services, they'd both be happy to know, I'm sure, that they're *almost* busier now than when they were alive! On any given day we field dozens of requests for film clips, memorial awards, memorabilia for charities, documentaries, television specials, movie deals, and countless licenses to merchandise rights . . . which we try to guide gracefully. Unfortunately, some of it translates into bizarre situations that neither Desi nor I enjoy dealing with very much.

I really hate coming into my office in the morning and

finding a full set of tiny *bobbing-head* dolls on my desk that look like some Hitchcock interpretation of Lucy Ricardo, with makeup by Salvador Dali. It's a lot to take in before you've had your coffee.

Sometimes you want to get on with your *own* life and not be forced to spend such enormous amounts of time talking about your deceased parents; to be continually liable for making responsible decisions on their behalf; to have to learn how to listen and decode all of the "shyster-meisters" who spend endless amounts of otherwise useful energy weaving weirder and weirder ways to snag their own personal piece of the "Lucy" legend.

And so many times you wish they *were* still here, even if for a few moments, just so you could turn around and ask, "Is this okay? Do you mind if they do this?" But you quickly realize that the voices that once could both calm your fears and drive you *so* crazy are truly silent forever. Until . . .

One day, while trying to sort out some of the complicated legalities of running the estates, Desi and I asked our mother's former attorney, Ed Perlstein, to sift through some of his old file boxes in search of some contracts we needed, and something remarkable happened!

There, in a dusty box of envelopes and tapes, he uncovered what turned out to be a never-before-published autobiographical work of our mother's. The package, postmarked 1966 from Betty Hannah Hoffman, Los Altos, California, simply said, LUCY. The manuscript was written in the first person, and seemed to span Mom's entire life up to 1964.

LOVE, LUCY

I was stunned. When I read it I cried. So many people, including myself, had tried to tell this story, but up until that moment I never knew that my mother had written about her own life. When my brother, Desi, read the manuscript he was overcome with emotions. He said, "I loved it. I *loved* reading it! There's wonderful energy that comes through . . . a fire in her belly, as a young kid, a sense of adventure. Like, 'I wanna make some noise.' Her connections from past to present . . . I salute her for her ability to think in terms of 'what did I learn from the past?' And there's some great straight-from-the-heart advice. I love the way she wrote about her feelings for Dad. It was very powerful for me to hear about when she first met him. Some people prolong their unhappiness by dramatizing it, which, as Vernon Howard used to tell me, was 'like expecting applause for having a headache.' Mom does *not* do this. Instead of overdramatizing what happened in her life, she seems to be trying to understand what her life is all about, to learn to love in a new way. That's what I found most endearing about this autobiography—the way she looked at life."

I have personally read hundreds of accounts of my mother's life over the years and thought I knew it all. But there were so many more *details* in this, especially regarding her earlier memories and what happened during her most formative years that contributed to the kind of woman, actress, and mother she became. I only wished I had had access to all of this priceless information in 1993, when I was making *Lucy and Desi: A Home Movie,* as it would have saved me a lot of time in research, and would have given me a much deeper understanding of the pain she had to assimilate as a child, and the depth of her struggle to achieve the kind of success she eventually did. Now, along with *A Book*, our father's fascinating, fact-filled reminiscence of *his* life, written in 1976, my brother and I and *our* children, along with the whole Ball-Arnaz clan, have one of the most remarkable, comprehensive family histories ever documented.

Another wonderful discovery was that Mrs. Hoffman had taped all her interviews with Mom, so although this is an "as told to" autobiography, unlike some others I have read, I could *hear* my mother's voice in the phrasing. Later, when I had the chance to listen to the twenty-some hours of original interviews, I realized that was because, for once in her life, my mother was quoted accurately!

I, of course, was tempted every now and then while editing to insert the note "See my father's book for *his* version of this same story"! But even then it was comforting to remember that there *are* always two sides to every story, and to take everyone's account of what happened to them with a grain of *salsa!*

So what happened, way back then, that put this *book* in that *box?*

I called Mom's longtime secretary, Wanda Clark, to see if *she* had any recollection of having worked on something like this, but Wanda was as shocked as I. The manuscript must have been tucked away shortly before she came to work for Mom.

I called my Aunt Cleo, who had been producing my

mother's radio shows around that same time, and who, at first, was as puzzled as Wanda had been, but who eventually said, "You know, I *do* have this memory of your mother talking into a tape recorder a lot." I called my stepfather, Gary, my mother's brother, Fred Ball, and longtime family friends like Marcella Rabwin, but no one knew anything about it. So I sent them all copies to help judge the manuscript's legitimacy and accuracy.

Even though they had known her longer than almost anyone, each in his or her own way found her autobiography "fascinating," "intriguing," and "illuminating," and marveled at her vivid recollections and the wealth of detail. And every one of them said something like, "Boy, you can really hear her voice in it!"

Finally, after many weeks of sleuthing, we were able to contact Mrs. Hoffman, now in her seventies and living in northern California, and as we tried to piece together the hows, wheres, and whens, we discovered some of the whys.

Apparently, in the early 1960s, not long after my mother had married Gary Morton, her dear friend and mentor, the late Dr. Norman Vincent Peale, encouraged her to record her thoughts about her dramatic and challenging life. But, knowing that she was starring in a television series, running a studio, and trying to raise two high-voltage teenagers at the same time, and would probably be unable to complete the task herself, he suggested she work *with* someone and do an "as told to"–type autobiography. I'm sure he must have convinced her that it would be historical *and* healing.

Mrs. Hoffman worked with my mother for about two years, taping and transcribing interview sessions. In addition to these sessions, she traveled to Mom's hometown of Jamestown, New York, interviewed her childhood friends, and then gave shape and order to the information.

Once given Mrs. Hoffman's name, people in my mother's circle began to recall the work's having taken place and remembered it as a difficult process. Aunt Cleo told me of one episode in particular. "I remember Betty used to come to me for help in figuring out ways to loosen your mother up and get her to tell the truth." I'm sure that one of my mother's motives for writing this was to set the record straight. Even by 1964, much had been written about her and my father that wasn't true. But I think in the beginning she was afraid that all Mrs. Hoffman would want to do was dwell on the "D" words (the drinking, the dames, and the divorce), and Mom was deeply concerned about hurting certain people who were still alive, especially my father, whom she still cared for very much. Aunt Cleo remembered that whenever Betty tried to get a more in-depth response, Mom would say, "Hell, if I talk about all that, I'll lose my General Foods image!" and Betty's smart retort, "Your 'General Foods image' is Jell-O, and I'm not writin' Jell-O!"

Betty was right. This ain't Jell-O. I was riveted. So why write something this good and then not let people read it?

My stepfather, Gary, remembers my mother's turning to him in bed one night to say that the book she was doing was upsetting her, that she "just couldn't finish it right now" because "it might hurt Desi."

L O V E ,   L U C Y

Robert Osborne of the *Hollywood Reporter* worked with my mother in the Desilu Workshop and recently told me that he *did* remember when she was working on the book. He recalls she was uncomfortable with writing an "autobiography" so soon because it made her feel as if the rest of her life wouldn't seem as important.

Whatever her reasons, all parties remember that the project was shelved with the understanding that everybody just forget about it, which is apparently what most people did.

Even in early April 1989, when my husband, Laurence Luckinbill, and I and our three children spent that Easter vacation with Mom and Gary in Palm Springs, she was telling us how she had "finally" agreed to begin work on an "as told to" autobiography for Putnam with her friend, and respected journalist, Bob Thomas. Either she had forgotten about the three-hundred-page "head start" she had lying around somewhere or she figured it would be easier to just start from scratch with someone entirely new. We'll never know, but I do remember how much she was dreading the April 1 deadline to start working with Bob.

She seemed completely overwhelmed by the task, couldn't imagine how or where to begin even. She no longer needed to fear hurting my father, since he had passed away two and a half years before, yet she feared *everything else:* that her memory wasn't sharp enough anymore, that "nobody would want to hear any of this stuff!" All the reminiscing was reminding her that a lot of the friends and loved ones, upon whom she would have liked to call for help, were no longer around.

Unfortunately, no one else had a chance to help her remember, either. She died less than three weeks later.

I remember thinking then how sadly ironic it was that my father should have gotten the chance to tell *his* story during his lifetime, but that we'd never get to hear Mom's—to see her life as she saw it. Sad for the family; sad for the world.

But since my mother *and* my father always insisted on a happy ending, I should have known. . . .

My brother, Desi, and I decided to share this with you now because we believe that's what she would have wanted, and inscribed it to all of you the way she would have signed it—simply, *Love, Lucy.*

So after all the rubber reproductions, the reruns, and the rag-sheet writings, after all those anemic imitations, and with her *impeccable* timing, she's come back . . . to speak for herself . . . in her *own* voice.

LUCIE ARNAZ

LOVE,
LUCY

Miss Lucille Ball
makes her debut
before the camera, 1911.

Chapter

1

♥

’m a Leo. I was born on a Sunday, August 6, 1911. Unfortunately, everybody knows my birth date because I told the truth when I first came to Hollywood.

I grew up not on the sidewalks of New York City, as some people think, but in the beautiful resort area of Lake Chautauqua, New York, near the green, wooded Allegheny wilderness.

I used to say I was born in Butte, Montana — I thought it sounded more glamorous than western New York. I was *conceived* in Montana when my father was working for his father as a lineman at Independent Telephone Company in Anaconda. But I was born in my grandparents' apartment on Stewart Street in Jamestown, New York, where I was delivered by my grandmother Flora Belle Hunt.

My mother, Desirée Hunt — or DeDe, as we call her — was of French-English descent, with a touch of Irish from her father's side that showed in her porcelain-fine English complexion and auburn hair. DeDe was so talented musically that she could have been a fine concert pianist, but at seventeen she met and married a local Jamestown boy, my father, Henry Durrell Ball. As soon after my birth as my mother could travel, she insisted we return to Montana and Henry.

Henry was tall, with intense, penetrating blue eyes. He was a wonderful guy, according to everyone who knew him: full of fun, with a good comic sense. DeDe says I got my sense of humor from him.

People are always asking me if Ball is my real name. As a young model, I tried being Diane Belmont for a while, but that kind of phony elegance wasn't for me. All I know about the Ball side of my family is that they are descended from an English family which owned houses and lands in Herefordshire in some early period. There were Ball mariners, hunters, priests, and barons, but, it appears, no actors. As for the American branch of the family, there was some Ball blood in George Washington; his mother's maiden name was Mary Ball. Ball family records place them in New York, Pennsylvania, Vermont, and Massachusetts, and I found gravestones of several Balls on Arthur Godfrey's farm in Virginia when we visited him last spring.

L O V E ,   L U C Y

For almost four years I was an only child. My young parents showered me with affection. I was at the center of the stage; life was a lark. DeDe tried dressing me in ribbons and bows, but I rebelled, never being the prissy doll type. My father roughhoused with me as he might with a boy, tossing me to the ceiling and catching me a few feet from the floor, and giving me piggybacks. I screamed with delight while DeDe worried about the tomboy she was raising.

I'm known among comediennes as a stunt girl who will do anything. Red Skelton flatters me by saying I have the courage of a tiger. I don't think it's a matter of bravery; it's just doing what comes naturally. I do know that if an actress has the slightest aversion to pie in the face or pratfalls, the camera will pick it up instantly. The audience won't laugh; they'll suffer in sympathy. Perhaps my willingness to be knocked off a twenty-foot pedestal or shot down a steamship funnel goes back to my earliest, happiest days with my father. I *knew* he was going to catch me; I *wasn't* going to get hurt.

DeDe says that I adored my young father. When I was about three, she got tired of the 40-below Montana winters and homesick for the gentle green hills of home, so eastward we went, to Wyandotte, Michigan, a suburb of Detroit, where my father became foreman of a telephone line crew.

Late one day the following January, my father caught the grippe and went to bed. Several days later a whopper of a sleet storm hit Detroit. Being a highly conscientious guy, my father bundled up to get the crews and payroll out. Despite his bad cough and fever, he climbed up poles in the sleet and snow, trying to secure the tangled, fallen wires. He kept going until the emergency was over, only to return to bed, this time with his fever raging.

My young mother was five months pregnant when my father fell ill. To keep me under control she tied me to a dog leash, which she then hitched to the clothesline in our backyard. Every time somebody would pass by on the sidewalk, I'd beg to be released. I must have been pretty convincing, because I was set free a lot. Then poor DeDe would have to frantically search the neighborhood for me.

My mother finally made arrangements with our kindly corner grocery store owner, Mr. Flower. He let me prance up and down his counter reciting little pieces my parents had taught me. My favorite was apparently a frog routine where I hopped up and down harrumphing. Then I'd gleefully accept the pennies or candy Mr. Flower's customers would give me — my first professional appearance!

My father's condition never improved. His grippe turned into typhoid fever. He died not long after that storm. He was only twenty-eight and my mother was almost twenty-three. I was not yet four, but I remember vividly the moment she told me Daddy was gone. I could tell you where the tables were, where the windows were, what they looked out on, where the bed was. And I remember at that very moment, a picture suddenly fell from the wall. And I noticed on the kitchen windowsill some little gray sparrows feeding.

I've been superstitious about birds ever since. I've heard that birds flying in the window are supposed to bring bad luck. I don't have a thing about live birds, but pictures of birds get me. I won't buy anything with a print of a bird, and I won't stay in a hotel room with bird pictures or bird wallpaper.

From Wyandotte, on a cold March morning, we returned to Jamestown with my father's coffin, and DeDe says I showed very little emotion until the funeral service. As they lowered his coffin into the ground and began filling in his grave, she says, I let out a bloodcurdling scream she'll never forget and wouldn't stop until she carried me away. After that, my mother and I returned to her parents' home in Jamestown. The next few years were very difficult ones for DeDe. She had practically no money and her parents had little to spare. I think she was a little stunned by her unhappy circumstances. I can remember her shaking her head, saying softly, "Married before I was eighteen, a mother before I was nineteen, and widowed before I was twenty-three." The future must have looked very bleak to her. She had been deeply in love with my father. I know she missed him very much.

DeDe's parents, my grandfather and grandmother Hunt, were then living in a small place on Buffalo Street in Jamestown. Their only son, my uncle Harold, had died of tuberculosis just a few years before, when he was only eighteen. They hadn't yet recovered from that loss, so when DeDe gave birth to a fine baby boy four months after my father's death, they were overjoyed. My brother arrived on Saturday, July 17, 1915, and was christened Fred Henry after Grandpa Hunt, who passed out cigars at the furniture factory that day and boasted to everyone about his fine boy, Freddy. He really thought of Freddy as his very own.

I was largely ignored and I became very jealous. It's always hard to go from being an only child to having an infant sibling in the house. Since my father had just died, I'm sure I was particularly sensitive to the great fuss that was made over the new baby. DeDe must have remembered that because, in 1953, when friends poured into our house with presents for little Desi, she stood by the front door and reminded them to "be sure to say hello to little Lucie first."

I remember feeling jealous about Freddy. But it, of course, wasn't his fault—he was a calm and levelheaded little boy, cooperative and hardworking. He took good care of all his belongings and never broke anything of mine. He never strayed far from home either, or caused anybody concern or worry. I was the tomboy and the daredevil, not Freddy. By the time I was twelve and Freddy was eight, I adored him, and have never changed my mind.

After Freddy's birth, my mother became more and more depressed, so finally it was decided that she should go to California for a complete change of scene. Freddy stayed with my mother's parents, while I was sent to live with my aunt Lola, my mother's younger sister. Lola was a plump, bosomy, easygoing woman who ran the best beauty shop in town. She had just married a Greek named George Mandicos.

George had been born and raised in Greece and spoke with an intriguing accent. He was the first Mediterranean type in my life, and he fascinated me. With my father dead, and me now separated from my mother, I naturally fell madly in love with Uncle George. My aunt and uncle were still honeymooning during this time. Distracted by each other, they couldn't have cared less whether I got to school or not. So most days I spent in my aunt's beauty shop or following Uncle George. Once again I was an only child, with a mother *and* a father, and it was such a happy, relaxed time for me.

DeDe, however, was miserable away from her children, so in a year or so, back she came to Jamestown. She'd been a widow for about three years when she married a big "ugly-handsome" Swede named Ed Peterson. He was a metal polisher, who enjoyed his home-brewed beer on Saturday night and took pride in his handsome wardrobe. Ed was known as a "dresser," and when he turned himself out, he looked like the King of Sweden. Ed was a pleasant guy to have around, but despite his marriage to our mother, he never thought of himself as a father to me and Freddy.

On DeDe's wedding day, I remember, I sidled up to the new groom, so thrilled to have a father again. "Are you our new daddy?" I smiled up at him.

Ed looked down at me with surprise. "Call me Ed," he said shortly, shaking his hand free of my viselike grip.

And that's the way it was. Ed was never mean or abusive, but his presence in the house was shadowy. We barely had time to get acquainted with him before he and DeDe went off to Detroit to look for jobs, leaving me and Freddy behind. My brother stayed with our doting grandparents, while I was parceled out to Ed's parents, the Petersons. Nothing had ever prepared me for such hard, sour, cheerless people. And since the Petersons were both quite elderly, I'm sure they were about as pleased as I was by our new living arrangements.

Having accepted the responsibility, Grandma Peterson was not one to shirk her duty. She had been born in Sweden, and her attitude toward the free and easy ways of America was one of distrust and suspicion. A devout Christian, she strove to keep her life and mine free of "indulgences." Anything that gave pleasure lapsed into one of the seven deadly sins and was therefore "devil's bait." Nothing in this life was ever to be enjoyed, only endured. Grandma Peterson took me to Sunday school regularly, and I remember a lot of talk of "fire and brimstone" there.

Punishments were frequent and, to me, unreasonable since I never got a satisfactory explanation of my crimes. My grandmother complained to the Hunts that I was difficult and headstrong. She told me that I was a "nervous child," and "sassy" and "bold" and "silly." And why not? I had so little outlet for my physical energies. My usual punishment was solitary confinement in my room or being sent to bed before the sun went down in summertime, when I could hear the happy shouts of other children playing outdoors.

Grandma Peterson saw to it that Satan found no mischief for my idle hands. She bought linen toweling by the yard and had me roll the edges by hand—finicky work that made me want to jump out of my skin. Another chore was darning the Peterson hose, which were as thick as a horse blanket. I was taught to knit and crochet. This last skill took. I still crochet with great enjoyment, everything from baby booties to coverlets for beds.

Washing dishes was a daily chore, and how I hated it! The kitchen was small and dark and the sink so high I had to stand on a box to reach it. The only light came from one weak gas jet; the water was heated on top of the stove and soon became lukewarm and greasy. After Grandmother Peterson inspected the finished job, she often made me start all over.

In retrospect, learning those domestic skills certainly didn't hurt me, and later on my own mother kept me at chores until I did them right. But where the Petersons made housework a grim chore, at the Hunts' we kids got a sense of cozy togetherness from pitching in.

There were some small advantages to the harsh, isolated life I led with the Petersons. I used to welcome a rainy day. Then I was allowed to play with my clothespin dolls in a corner of the back porch. I can close my eyes and still see the leaden sky, the rain splashing off the porch roof, the bright green maple leaves clinging together like wet crepe paper, and I can hear my involved conversations with those dolls.

Curiously enough, Grandmother Peterson had a green thumb, and I have her to thank for my great love for flowers, especially spring flowers. Somewhere inside her there must have been a well of maternal tenderness which found expression in the way she pruned and prayed over and tended her roses, her prize dahlias, the bulbs she brought indoors during the winter and set out again in the spring.

I don't suppose that hard work, discipline, and a perfectionist attitude toward my work did me any harm. They are a big part of my makeup today, as any of my co-workers will tell you. And when life seemed unbearable, I learned to live in my imagination, and to step inside other people's skins—indispensable abilities for an actress. On the other hand, I have my grandmother Peterson to thank for the gnawing sense of unworthiness and insecurity that haunted me for years. The Puritan idea that everything pleasurable is somehow bad almost ruined for me the first joys of our big *I Love Lucy* success. The hardest thing for me was getting used to the idea that I deserved it.

I went back to visit the Petersons on many later occasions, and I finally realized that in her strange way, Ed's mother was actually fond of me, despite her strict old-country ways.

When DeDe and Ed returned from Detroit, Grandfather Hunt decided to buy a place in the country so we could all live together under the same roof. On February 1, 1920, Fred P. Hall and Lucy M. Hall deeded to Fred C. Hunt and Flora B. Hunt for the sum of $2,000 our new home on Eighth Street in Celoron! Boy, were we excited!

I was so grateful to have a mother again. I never went through a critical "Oh, Mother!" stage with DeDe. I always knew that she was on my side. It never occurred to me to talk back or argue. Over the years, I have always treasured her advice, which is salty, sensible, and never one-sided. Having her back again was just about the greatest thing that ever happened to me.

DeDe still feels guilty about the time we were apart, but I understand that circumstances forced our separation, and she certainly has made up for it with unflagging devotion ever since. When we speak of the slights of our childhood, it's hard to remember that often people were struggling to do their level best. This knowledge comes to you later in life, of course, when you have children of your own.

Once we were all back together again with Grandma and Grandpa Hunt, everything straightened out magically. DeDe still had to work full-time, but my grandparents were home quite a lot. I have them to thank for most of the happy times of my childhood.

My grandfather Hunt began life as the only son of a well-to-do Jamestown hotel owner. Grandpa Hunt worked in his father's hotel, then ran a grocery store in Jamestown, and was also a postman, a maker of optical instruments, and a chiropractor. Some people called him "Doctor" from his brief brush with that last calling. He kept his old chiropractor's leather couch, and neighbors soon learned how his strong fingers could ease an aching back. He was also a skilled wood turner. When I was quite young, this is how he earned his living in one of Jamestown's fine furniture plants.

Grandfather Fred had a jaunty air about him, with bright blue eyes and sandy hair that kept its color even into his seventies. He was at once cunning, cute, cocky, and wonderfully good to us kids.

He met and married my grandmother, Flora Belle Orcutt, when she was a chambermaid in his father's hotel. The

Orcutts had farmed for several generations in the rolling green countryside around Charlotte Center, a crossroads about twenty miles from Jamestown. They were strong, sturdy folk with the earthy good sense that comes from tending animals and tilling the soil. I can still remember some of those wonderful meals we had around the Orcutts' groaning board.

Flora Belle was one of five sets of twins and was orphaned at an early age. At one time, the children were about to be sent to an orphanage, and Flora Belle, although she was not the oldest, lost no time in getting all her nine brothers and sisters under the same roof. They've all held her in great respect.

Grandmother Flora Belle was very beautiful, with good bone structure, curly salt-and-pepper hair, a trim figure, and good legs. Her hands were also very shapely, with long fingers, but red and roughened from hard work and the strong solutions she used as a practical nurse. She was just about the best midwife in Jamestown and was much in demand. Flora Belle was a dedicated nurse with a very open, welcoming attitude toward the world. Always cooking, cleaning, sewing, she was a sunny, active, vigorous woman, a dreamer and a planner. Nothing was too much for her, no hours too long, no time better spent than doing things for her family.

Grandmother Hunt didn't have much formal education—and she hung on Grandfather's every word. He was the bookish type, interested in words and their derivations, and fond of reading aloud. Sometimes it was poetry, and sometimes politics, or a book like *Black Beauty*, which he read to us kids.

Grandmother would come into the room and sit quietly sewing as she listened. I remember the scratchy sound her work-roughened fingers made as she handled scraps of silk for her quilts. Sometimes, if the story he read was a sad one, tears would slip down her soft cheeks, falling on the silk in her lap.

My grandparents had little money, but they gave us a richly satisfying family life.

I was eight and a half years old when we all moved into the little three-bedroom house on Eighth Street in Celoron, which held first two and then three families. I loved every inch of that weathered shingled house. It had a front porch and a back shed, and a small, dark front parlor separated from the front hall by portieres. These were the stage curtains for our innumerable productions as Freddy and I grew up.

My bedroom was in the rear, overlooking the big backyard with its high hedge of purple lilacs. My bureau had three drawers. The bottom drawer was filled with stage costumes. Old bedspreads, discarded curtains, bits of chicken feathers, ribbon, and lace all found their way into that drawer and were happily put to use.

No sooner were both families cozily under one roof than Aunt Lola gave birth to a daughter—with the expert help of Grandmother Flora Belle. Since Aunt Lola had a beauty shop to run, her daughter, Cleo, stayed with us and became our baby. Cleo had great dark eyes, black curly hair, plump dimpled little knees, and her mother's good humor. As soon as she could walk, she was added to our "repertory company." I would dress her, make her up, and rehearse her lines with her. Since all the adult members of the household worked, I seldom went anywhere without Freddy hanging on to one hand and Cleo the other.

For as jealous as I was of Freddy at his birth, it wasn't long before I'd completely taken him under my wing. Not only was he a levelheaded and hard working little boy, he was an amiable costar in all our homespun productions.

Many of the inspirations for our stage plays came from the fine productions we saw on summer evenings at Celoron Amusement Park, which was just a hop, skip, and a jump from our house across a daisy field and a railroad track. The park was built by the owners of Jamestown's worsted mills and street railways at the turn of the century. To us, it was as unique and wonderful as Disneyland is today, with its calliope, Ferris wheel, and merry-go-round. Many wealthy Pittsburgh oil families built summer homes on Lake Chautauqua, and DeDe could remember when they came to the park dressed to the teeth, riding shiny carriages with matched chestnuts and liveried grooms. Back then there was a lake steamer which brought in boatloads from the world-famous Chautauqua In-stitute at the northern end of the lake.

Sousa performed in the bandshell, and Pauline MacLain performed in *Mrs. Wiggs of the Cabbage Patch* in the summer. She stayed in a rented house in Celoron. I used to hang around outside, hoping to catch a glimpse of my idol. One morning she threw open the window and stood there, shaking out her sheets and blankets, in curlers and a dust cap. That was a disillusioning sight.

LOVE, LUCY

There was no admission fee to the park, and any summer evening we could stroll over and watch the fountains of colored water or the spectacular fireworks or see *The Perils of Pauline* on the flickering outdoor screen. A man named Rex who sported black tights made balloon ascensions in a little basket. After hovering for a while he'd parachute into the park and sometimes, if the wind was strong, into the lake. When its load of gas was spent, the balloon would come down, and there was a reward for anyone who found it. I can still picture it streaking down from the sky like a long black cigar.

Celoron got its name from a French explorer, a Comte de Céloron. In the late eighteenth century, he paddled down the twenty-mile Lake Chautauqua and landed at the southern end of the lake, which thereafter was known as Celoron. Next the British claimed the land, and then the Americans. Most of the early settlers in the area came from New England.

This Puritan heritage is deep in my blood; my dearest dream is to live in a little white house in New England with a lilac bush by the front door. My husband, Gary, calls me "one of the Eskimo people." He dotes on sunshine and hot weather and hates the snow and ice. We really had blizzards in Celoron; the lake froze solid a mile across and was covered with ice-skaters and iceboats and ice fishermen. I'd love to live in New England, where I could have that bright clear air and clean snow and change of seasons.

There's another New England thing about me, and that's a strong conservative, Puritan streak. I've always known right from wrong and I'd like to know how I learned this, to make sure my kids do. I'm the most conservative member of my family. Grandfather Freddy was a progressive and a free-thinker; DeDe was a product of the Roaring Twenties. She believed in letting go and expressing yourself; bang your fist and let your feelings out. She never gave a fig what other people said or thought.

My mother gave us kids freedom and was permissive. DeDe says she knew what stuff we were made of and trusted us. I do know that growing up right next to an amusement park can be very bad. Some of the kids ran wild there; and although I appreciated the magic of the place and the spell of make-believe it cast, it's hard to develop a real sense of values growing up next to a commercial carnival. But apparently I profited from the experience. I am not easily taken in by anyone.

The little red brick Celoron schoolhouse which we attended from kindergarten through high school was just half a block from our house. I was lucky to grow up in a regular little United Nations: kids of old Anglo-Saxon stock and kids whose fathers or grandfathers came from Italy, Albania, Greece, Germany, Poland, Norway, Sweden, and Denmark. Jamestown is a great furniture center, and skilled wood-workers came there from all over the world, so many of my classmates had fathers who were highly skilled craftsmen. Like my grandfather, they took great pride in their work.

Grandfather had a little workshop at home, where he made us all kinds of things. He built us sleds and wagons and wheelbarrows, and stilts, pogo sticks, swings, teeter-totters, and treehouses. And just for me he made the most absolutely marvelous doll furniture, some of which I still treasure. Using fine pieces of cherry and walnut and mahogany, he turned and scrolled the tiny posts of doll beds and chair legs.

Gradually, mass production methods displaced the old slow, careful, finicky ways of making fine furniture. My grandfather learned to run a lathe, but he missed the satisfaction of transforming a piece of wood into something of elegance and beauty with his own hands. He wound up as a factory worker before the days of the unions and saw many abuses of authority. And because he was an idealist, a sincere humanitarian, he became a follower of Socialist leader Eugene Debs, the fiery defender of all underdogs.

I remember the glorious day in Celoron when the indoor bathtub arrived. We already had an indoor bathroom with a toilet, to put it indelicately, but no tub since we had no hot water. Saturday-night baths meant heating the water on the big iron wood-burning kitchen stove. When we were small, I got first turn in the galvanized washtub, followed by Freddy. In the summertime, Grandfather wouldn't let us go swimming in Lake Chautauqua without taking along a cake of soap for shampooing our hair and washing all over. So we really felt like celebrating when hot water and a tub finally arrived. It was a new luxury to soak and scrub in privacy.

We kids always called Grandfather Hunt "Daddy," and kept calling him that to the end of his days. He *was* our daddy in the sense that he was the man of the household, whom we loved and obeyed. He was great on discipline and if you didn't hop to it at once, *wham!* you got it. Once I dillydallied too long getting to the dinner table and Daddy spanked me with the gravy spoon—with gravy still on it! There was hot chicken gravy all over the dining room and my Sunday dress, too.

The great thing about my grandfather Hunt was that he took such good care of everything. He taught us the same pride of ownership. Once I slid down the coal bin in the cellar, tearing my dress and ruining my white shoes with coal dust. I really got it good. That cellar was a fascinating place to me: mysterious, and at the same time so planned and orderly. There were the empty boxes left over from one Christmas waiting for the next, the fragrance of freshly cut wood, rows of Grandmother's canning, the damp smell of the earth floor. Eggs were kept in a pottery crock. It was kind of spooky reaching down into the cold brine, getting wet to the elbow. And those damn spiders, how I hated them! Snakes would crawl in there too. "Look," Daddy would say, picking one up, "it's just a garter snake, don't you see? He's harmless." Of course, there were rattlesnakes and copperheads in the area, and he taught us to recognize them, too, as he taught us to know the poisonous kinds of mushrooms.

Daddy's truck garden drew admirers for miles around. He kept us in fresh vegetables and berries all summer, and the rest was canned for good eating all during the long, hard winters. During the cold weather the cat always gave birth to a litter of kittens in the cellar and hid them down there. Then some evening when we were all upstairs she would cry at the cellar door. When one of us let her out, she'd carry her brood up one by one, by the scruff of the neck, so we could admire them.

While Cleo was still a baby, Grandmother Flora Belle gave up a lot of her nursing jobs and stayed home to look after her. But then Grandmother's health began to fail, and looking after the younger kids and getting supper on the table became my responsibility.

I couldn't understand why Grandmother's nerves would sometimes snap—but her pain and our racket must have been unbearable at times. DeDe said that I had to practice the piano for one hour every afternoon after school. She was a wonderful pianist and insisted that I had music in me—and that's where it stayed: in me. Grandmother used to encourage me to practice too, but once she fell ill, my playing only seemed to irritate her.

I just couldn't understand the change in my beloved grandmother. Then one day I learned that she had uterine cancer and wasn't going to get well. She got weaker and weaker. Toward the end, she lay all the time in her big mahogany bed in the front parlor.

Grandmother Hunt wasted away. When she died, released at last from her suffering, I was not allowed to go to the funeral. I took little Cleo and Freddy by the hand and followed the funeral procession down the street, crying my heart out. Grandmother Hunt was only fifty-one when she died. Because of her, I have a special place in my heart for cancer research. Although she knew her own case was hopeless, she prayed to the end for a cure for others.

♥

Each Memorial Day we would cut great branches of blooming lilacs from the purple bushes in the backyard and carry them to Lakeview Cemetery to Grandmother's grave. Since those days, lilac has become almost an obsession with me; someone once interpreted my passion for it as signaling a return to the womb, to Celoron, to the innocent happiness of childhood. Whatever the reason, the emotional tug is so overwhelming that I've been known to plan trips to New England in May just to see and smell lilac in bloom. It's difficult to grow in California, although I've been trying for many years. There are actually male and female bushes, although nobody seems able to tell them apart. We just plant them all together in the sunniest corner of the garden and hope. This year they bloomed for the very first time. They don't have the fragrance of lilacs in the East, of course. Still, I was delighted!

After Grandmother Hunt died, there was no adult in the house during the day. I suddenly found myself in her shoes, at the age of eleven. Freddy was then seven, and Cleo three.

DeDe was certainly a powerful example of a woman's dedication to her family. She could seldom get home from her job selling hats until six or six-thirty, including Saturdays. So it was my job to make the beds, do the dusting, make sure the table was set, cook dinner, and do the supper dishes. Then DeDe would be up past midnight scrubbing and ironing clothes, mending and sewing. She had two dresses to her name, both black, which she kept brushed and clean, and wore with white collars or pearls. At this time, DeDe was thirty, still a handsome woman, with an infectious laugh.

Selling hats was tedious work. My mother was on her feet long hours, and the pay was low. She never complained, and always put on a good front, but we knew how the fatigue and worry of making ends meet aggravated her excruciating migraine headaches. I'm a headache sufferer myself, so I know what she went through, but luckily for me, today headaches can be better controlled.

I can still see DeDe now, on Sunday afternoons, parceling her weekly earnings into little envelopes. There would be $1.25 for insurance, or $4 for a new clothes washer, or $2 for a new set of porch furniture, everything bought on time. But I had the most beautiful clothes of any kid in school. I was always the first with the latest, be it a raccoon coat, open galoshes, or the blue serge middy blouse to go with my short, boyish bob. DeDe always wanted the best for her children, even if it meant going into hock to pay for it.

Every afternoon we'd telephone her at Marcus's, the elegant dress shop where she worked in Jamestown. As soon as she heard we were all safely home from school, she'd hang up. Then we'd playact the rest of the afternoon, until we saw DeDe step off the trolley at the end of the street. Then Freddy would rush to set the table, and I'd throw together the beds. Then I'd get out the dust mop. When DeDe walked in, she'd first look up the stairwell to see how many clouds of dust were still dancing in the light. I don't remember her ever being upset about it, but she'd have some remark that let us know we hadn't fooled anyone. I missed not having her around all the time—that day-to-day closeness I try to give my own children—but even then I understood why this was just not possible.

About this time, when I was eleven or twelve, I tried my first cigarette. DeDe came into my little back bedroom and found it blue with smoke. "Oh, so you're smoking now," she remarked pleasantly. "Let's have one together." She kept me inhaling one cigarette after another, until I turned purple and then green. I was eighteen before I tried smoking again.

Aunt Lola often let me help out in her beauty shop. I'd operate on the customers' children, frizzing their hair with a smoking-hot marcel iron and nicking their ears with the shingling shears. I think I actually put Aunt Lola out of business. The children's irate mothers just refused to come near the place. Ultimately Aunt Lola closed up shop and went into nursing. However, I still love everything about the beauty business. I have a roomful of hairdressing equipment and give permanents, hair sets, manicures, and pedicures to this day. Only now, I'm good at it.

When she left to enter nurse's training, Aunt Lola also got a divorce from my uncle George. He moved away and out of our lives, and Cleo stayed with us. She was a cuddly, affectionate child, who often crawled into DeDe's bed or lap to be comforted. Our pet name for her was "Cleo-baby"; Freddy was "Fritzie-boy"; I was "Lucille-what-the-hell-are-you-doing-now?"

Among the things that made life interesting in Celoron were the train wrecks. The Erie tracks ran around the lake from Mayville, the county seat to the north, and passed just a few hundred yards from our house. One day Mrs. Curtis, the only wealthy member of our community, got stuck on the tracks in her electric car. She lived in a big stucco house which took up a whole block, surrounded by a high fence. She was a mysterious person to us kids, since we knew so little about her.

Apparently she was slightly deaf, for she never heard the train coming before the collision. The car was demolished but Mrs. Curtis, merely injured. The train conductors loaded her into the baggage car and chugged off to Jamestown and the hospital.

At the scene of the wreck, I found some amber beads. I toyed with the idea of keeping them, but in the end, honesty prevailed. After Mrs. Curtis got home from the hospital, I marched through her impressive front gate and rang the door-bell. She turned out to be a sweet and charming lady. She gave me the most thrilling gift I had ever received—a reward for returning the beads: a real gold wristwatch.

Another time an Erie freight car became uncoupled and rode up over the flatcar in front; there was a tremendous crash and sound of splintering wood as twenty-five freight cars toppled off the track. People came pouring out of their homes and so did I, but not empty-handed. I bounded across the field with a bucket of water in each hand. No homeless tramp was going to burn up in one of those freight cars if I could help it.

Being the eldest, I had to keep track of the two younger kids. Luckily, they were both easy to manage and sel-dom got into mischief. DeDe really loaded me with heavy re-sponsibilities, but more important, she trusted me to make the right decisions. My childhood was challenging, but not back-breaking. DeDe set the challenges, and I pretty much met them and grew stronger.

People with happy childhoods never overdo; they don't strive or exert themselves. They're moderate, pleasant, well-liked, and good citizens. Society needs them. But the tremendous drive and dedication necessary to succeed in *any* field—not only show business—often seems to be rooted in a disturbed childhood. I wasn't an unloved or an unwanted child, but I was moved around a lot, and then death and cruel circumstances brought many painful separations.

My adolescence was about as stormy as you might imagine. I had a redheaded temper (though no red hair) in those days. Cleo remembers me as a creative, strong-willed teenager, whirling like a pinwheel. I can remember kicking, rolling, biting fights on the school grounds; there were some girls I certainly had some rounds with, and a few boys, too. There was an Italian typing teacher I was crazy about, but once she made me so mad I threw a typewriter at her.

It takes me a long time to get angry, but when I do it's such a compilation of things over a long period that nobody can quite understand what triggered it finally . . . even myself.

There's a great deal of difference between tempera-ment and temper. Temperament is something you welcome creatively, for it is based on sensitivity, empathy, aware-ness . . . but a bad temper takes too much out of you and doesn't really accomplish anything.

*In her restless teens,
Lucille was already beginning
to look beyond Jamestown,
circa 1925.*

Chapter

2

♥

When I got to be thirteen, a lot of pressures that had been building up for years suddenly found expression. Most of my stunts were the kind of silly antics most teenagers do to draw attention to themselves. On a dare, I roller-skated on the freshly varnished school gymnasium floor . . . tore through Celoron sitting on the front radiator of a boy's tin lizzie . . . And I ran away a lot. I'd leave the classroom for a drink of water and never come back.

Looking back, I think my main need was for somebody to talk to, to confide in, some wise and sympathetic older person. My school principal, Bernard Drake, became such a per-

son. Mr. Drake was the first person to label my exuberant feelings as talent and to urge me to go on the stage. In the eighth
grade, I had many long, satisfying talks with him. Then he left
Celoron to work at a state normal school. I missed him so
much that one day I took little Cleo by the hand and we hitch-
hiked fifty miles to his new home. He called DeDe and had us
on a bus the next morning.

The summer that I was fourteen an immense restless-
ness swept over me. Things weren't going too well at home.
DeDe and Ed got divorced five or six years later, but the first
real fights and arguments started at about this time. My
mother's face grew pinched with worry and often a taxi would
bring her home from the store in the middle of the afternoon,
suffering one of her migraine headaches. She would lie in a
darkened room with the shades down, unable to move or talk,
until the attack passed. I worried about her and the hard life
she led.

Grandpa Hunt wasn't too happy either, running his
lathe at Crescent Tool. Ever since Grandmother Flora Belle
died, he seemed torn loose from his moorings. It made him mad
that the factory workers shared little of the great prosperity
then sweeping the country. This, of course, was long before
the days of Social Security or unemployment benefits; when
a man lost his job, his family could starve, and a serious illness
could bankrupt him for life.

All the local kids got summer jobs at the amusement
park; I was hired as a short-order cook at a hamburger stand.
I took my job seriously and loved earning the money. "Look

out! Look out! Don't step *there*!" I'd suddenly holler at some person passing by, and as he stopped, startled, one foot in midair and looking worriedly at the ground, I'd continue: "Step over *here* and get yourself a de-licious hamburger!" This mesmerized a lot of people into buying, and incidentally, they were darn good hamburgers.

DeDe kept a strict check on me, and I had to be home at a certain time each night. I wasn't allowed to go out in any canoes. The one time I decided to live dangerously and went canoeing with a boy, I had to tip it over to get back. I got wet but was still virtuous!

DeDe had to force me to go to my first dance at the Celoron Pier Ballroom. They still had all the big-name bands, like Harry James and Glenn Miller and Benny Goodman. DeDe let me wear lipstick, and she made me a perfectly beautiful dress of pussy willow taffeta with a band of real fur around the bottom. A girl at the dance wearing some stale dress oohed and aahed over it and then asked, "Can I have it?" The next day I gave it to her. DeDe was furious, and I don't blame her. But this girl came from a very large, poor family and never had any nice things.

But the most momentous thing that happened to me during my fourteenth summer was that I fell in love. I never laugh at puppy love, or shrug it off; my kids are going through their first wild crushes, and I know how they can hurt. Anyway, DeDe was away most of the time at the store, Ed paid little attention to us, and Daddy spent most of his spare time with Freddy. Maybe I was still searching for a father; maybe

Johnny reminded me of another Mediterranean type I had once been crazy about, my uncle George. Whatever the reason, the summer I was almost fifteen, I fell deeply in love with an Italian boy of twenty-three.

Johnny Davita had a John Garfield build, but his features were finely chiseled and his dark eyes warm and full of life. He came from a large, prosperous Jamestown family and was studying to be a doctor when I first met him.

At first my nutty antics made him laugh. Then we danced together at the ballroom. He was very sweet and protective toward me. Mainly we talked. I wanted to share with him everything that had ever happened to me, and all my hopes for the future. I had no thought of being an actress then; I just wanted to be *somebody*, and to make things easier for DeDe.

When my friend Pauline Lopus and I went back to the little red schoolhouse in Celoron in the fall of 1926 as high school freshmen, we were the only girls in the school with boyish bobs. This inspired us to put on our first amateur production, *Charley's Aunt.* I had a wonderful teacher that year, Miss Lillian Appleby, who, like Mr. Drake, tried to channel my driving urge to express myself into acting.

DeDe never tried to hem me in. Be an actress? Sure, why not? She sat up until midnight many nights sewing her eyes out, making us costumes, and was in charge of many school productions.

DeDe didn't turn a hair when we hauled to the school stage all the brown wicker living room furniture she was still buying on time. When my stepfather got home from work, he raised Cain. "There's no place to sit!" he protested. DeDe shrugged. "We'll sit on the front porch in the swing till the play is over," she told him.

For the most part, Ed encouraged my acting. But I don't think a stage career ever occurred to me until one night when he took me to see the great monologuist Julius Tannen in the Celoron school auditorium. This virtuoso sat in a chair on a bare stage with a single light over his head and transported us wondrously. (Recently, I had a chance to meet Mr. Tannen and tell him what an important part he played in my getting into the business.)

With *Charley's Aunt,* I knew for the first time that wonderful feeling that comes from getting real laughs on a stage. I not only played the male lead, but sold the tickets, swept up the stage afterward, and turned out the lights.

The night of the first performance, Pauline stood at the entrance to the school auditorium collecting the tickets. She barely had time to dash backstage and throw on her long Victorian skirts and her bonnet before I yanked the curtain up. She started to speak her opening lines, then stopped, and a funny expression came over her face.

"What's the matter?" I hissed. "Forget your lines?"

"No," said Pauline with great annoyance. "I forgot my *makeup*!"

This was the main reason she wanted to be in the play: the chance to use real makeup with her mother's approval.

Charley's Aunt was a great success. We charged twenty-five cents a ticket, and made twenty-five dollars, and gave all of it to the ninth grade for a class party. Pauline and I often recall the thrill that gave us. She still lives in the same little house in Celoron and is now a dedicated guidance counselor, who never stops learning and giving.

The success of *Charley's Aunt* encouraged me to get into as many musical and dramatic offerings as I could, from the school drama club to the Shriners' annual productions. I even bounced up on the stage of the Palace Theater in Jamestown to be photographed by some traveling shyster who had fallen heir to an old camera and some bad film. That was my first moving picture—something called *Tillie the Toiler*.

When I was fifteen, the Harry F. Miller Company put on a musical called *The Scottish Rite Revue* on that same Palace stage. I did an Apache dance with such fervor that I fell into the orchestra pit and pulled an arm out of its socket. The *Jamestown Post Journal* hailed me as "a new discovery," and the head of the Jamestown Players, Bill Bemus, told me I was "chock-full of talent."

That summer I worked at the park at an ice cream stand and danced through the starry summer nights with Johnny. DeDe disapproved of my romance with him. She felt he was too old for me, and she was troubled by rumors surrounding Johnny's father and the mob. This was the lawless twenties, the era of the Untouchables, Al Capone, and Prohibition. Technically, everyone who touched alcohol was a lawbreaker: the guy who ran the booze in from Canada and the guy who bought it from him illegally. I thought Prohibition was a silly and impractical law, and so did most people at the time, even DeDe. But my mother didn't want me involved with anyone who might be deemed unsavory.

Prohibition had a bad effect on Celoron, for with the closing of all public bars, the great resort hotels ringing the lake began to die on their feet. Some were boarded up, others torn down. When the fine restaurants and hotels disappeared, the wealthy oil families from Pittsburgh began to go elsewhere and their big houses stood empty. Beautiful Celoron Amusement Park began to go slightly downhill. It was never a Coney Island—there were no barkers or cheap sideshows—but gradually, the type of people strolling through the park and doing business there changed.

I was much too busy working to pay much attention. I had a few brushes with disaster. I had to run like hell to get out of the way of somebody rolling out of a speakeasy, but just once or twice.

Early one morning, Johnny wasn't as lucky: His father was shot and killed in front of the Catholic church as he came out of six-o'clock mass. Johnny's ambition to be a doctor died with his father. From then on, he was head of his family, with a mother and many siblings to support.

DeDe asked Johnny to stay away from me. It didn't do much good, although, in my heart, I must have known she was right. Eventually, given her opposition and Johnny's new responsibilities, he and I saw less and less of each other. But our love was the real thing: it remained a love that haunted me for many years—at least until I came to Hollywood.

♥

The summer following my sophomore year at high school, they held a Miss Celoron bathing beauty contest at the park. Miss America of 1927 was to be the judge, and it was quite a big deal locally.

I didn't particularly want to be in a bathing beauty contest. I was very skinny, being my present height of five feet seven and a half but weighing less than a hundred pounds. And I had freckles on my back, which embarrassed me terribly. But somebody entered my name, so I went along with it. The feminine ideal at this time was Clara Bow with her heart-shaped face and short ringlets. I tried my darnedest to look like Clara Bow—but to no avail. The candidates were supposed to have their pictures in the paper before the contest, and DeDe sent me to the best photographer in Jamestown, T. Henry Black. It was Mr. Black who was quoted as saying, "It's very difficult to get a satisfactory picture of Miss Ball because the lady is just *not* photogenic!"

I think I was runner-up in the contest, but what I remember most is my embarrassment. Only recently have I begun wearing bathing suits again.

Right after the beauty contest came the Fourth of July, the real start of my sixteenth summer and the biggest weekend at the amusement park. My grandfather Fred, in a holiday mood, came home from work on the trolley with a mysterious object wrapped in brown paper. It was a birthday present for Freddy who was about to turn twelve—a real

.22-caliber rifle. Freddy wanted to shoot crows right away, but Daddy told him, "You can't use it until tomorrow, Fritzie-boy. Tomorrow I'll show you how."

Early the next morning the crowds began piling off the trolley and heading toward the lake, with picnic baskets, and the small fry waving little red-white-and-blue flags. It was a bright sunny July day, and the heavy scent of clover floated from the meadow which stretched between us and the railroad tracks. I was in a hurry to get to my hamburger job at the park, but I hung around for a while to watch the gun lesson. Although Cleo and Freddy were big kids now, I still thought of them as my charges.

Daddy set up a tin-can target in our backyard and then in his usual meticulous, careful way explained all about the gun. Besides me and Freddy, there were Cleo and Johanna, a girl Freddy's age who was visiting someone in the neighborhood. Daddy placed the tin can about forty feet away, in the direction of some open fields where there were no houses.

There was an eight-year-old boy who lived at the corner whose name was Warner Erickson. Every once in a while you would hear his mother shriek, "War-ner! Get home!" and Warner would streak for his yard since his mother spanked him for the slightest infraction. This Fourth of July weekend he had wandered into our yard and was peeking around the corner of our house watching the target practice. We didn't notice him at first, but then Daddy told him, "Now Warner, please sit down and stay out of the way." Warner moved close to us and obediently sat down on the grass to watch. My friend Pauline was also watching from a safe distance, on her back stoop.

My brother was shooting at the target, and then it was his little girlfriend's turn. Johanna picked up the gun and held it against her shoulder with one eye closed. At that moment, we heard a strident, "War-*ner*, get home this minute!"

Warner darted in the direction of his home, right in front of the rifle. The gun went off and Warner fell spread-eagled to the ground, into the lilac bushes.

"I'm shot! I'm shot!" Warner screamed.

"No you're not," said Daddy. "Get up."

Then we saw the spreading red stain on Warner's shirt, right in the middle of his back.

Cleo screamed, and I took her in my arms. Warner was exactly her age and was her special playmate. The slam of a screen door told me that Pauline was running to tell her mother. Daddy looked stunned; then he picked up Warner as gently as a leaf. He talked to him in a low, comforting voice. The girl who had fired the gun was in shock.

The balloon ascension was beginning at the park. You could see it drifting up above the trees to the burst of applause below. Warner was quiet in Daddy's arms as we all walked the hundred yards to his house.

Then Warner's mother burst out of her back door. At the sight of the blood and her son's slack body, she began screaming hysterically. There was a long, long wait for the ambulance. While we huddled together in a frightened group,

Mrs. Erickson raced up and down the street telling everyone, "They've shot my son! They've shot my son!"

The next few days were a kind of nightmare as we all hung on to bulletins from the hospital. Then we learned the awful news: a .22-caliber bullet is very small, but by fantastic bad luck, the bullet passed right through Warner's spine, severing the cord.

One of my first scrapbooks contains a yellowed clipping from the *Post-Journal* of July 5, 1927: "Warner Erickson, eight years old, of Celoron, is still in critical condition at Jamestown General Hospital as a result of being shot in the back Sunday, July 3, at Celoron. Lucille and Fred Ball were shooting at a target at the rear of their home. The Erickson lad stepped out in the range as Johanna Ottinger, a young girl, fired at about the same time, the bullet entering the boy's back and passing through his lungs, lodging in the chest. Mr. Hunt, grandfather of the Ball children, was watching the target practice."

In a week or so, Warner came home from the hospital. His mother often wheeled him up and down the sidewalk in front of our house. Each time Cleo saw him, she started to cry. We were all terribly fond of Warner.

Daddy would have gladly paid Warner's doctors' bills the rest of his life, but the Ericksons didn't come to see Daddy; they went to a lawyer. They planned to sue Daddy for everything he had, they told the whole neighborhood. Feelings ran hot and high, pro and con. Daddy couldn't believe anyone could even *think* it was anything but an accident. The possibility of a lawsuit worried him greatly. He was then sixty-two and near the end of his working career. His tiny life savings and the house were all he had to face the future. So on the advice of a lawyer he deeded the house over to his daughters, DeDe and Lola, for payment of one dollar.

It was almost a year before the case came to trial in the county civil court. Daddy was charged with negligence since he had been the only adult present. It was a muggy, overcast day in May 1928, the lilacs in full heady bloom, when Daddy's lawyer drove us to the imposing yellow courthouse in Mayville, at the northern end of the lake. The Colonial-style courtroom was large and imposing, with light wood paneling and impressive oil portraits around the room, of judges in their somber robes.

The Ericksons wheeled in young Warner and parked him right in front of the jury box so that everybody could get a good look at him. Two Jamestown doctors who had attended him testified how the bullet had entered his spine. Warner was paralyzed from the waist down for life, they said. He sat listening with bright, intelligent eyes. I was trembling and feeling sick to my stomach; Daddy was white as a sheet.

My grandfather didn't have many witnesses in his defense: just DeDe, Freddy, Cleo, and me. The visiting girl who fired the shot, Johanna Ottinger, wasn't there. Her testimony might have helped Daddy a great deal but she was home in another state. In fact, none of us ever saw her again.

Cleo cried on the witness stand, and Freddy and I, scared half to death, stuttered and stammered as we stated and restated all the precautions Daddy had taken; how Warner, uninvited, had been told to sit on the grass at a safe distance and not to move; and how he had suddenly popped up at the sound of his mother's voice and darted in front of the gun.

The trial began one afternoon and continued into the next morning. Someone got on the witness stand and said that Daddy had made a *target* out of Warner and let us practice on him. We couldn't believe our ears. How could anyone possibly blame Daddy for the accident? It was just an inexplicable tragedy.

The jury went out about eleven o'clock in the morning and was gone for four and a half hours. We paced up and down the courthouse corridors for what seemed an eternity. Then the jury solemnly filed back and we learned that the Ericksons had won their case. Daddy had been negligent, they said, and he must pay the Ericksons $4,000, although all the gold in the world couldn't restore Warner's ability to walk.

Now, this doesn't seem like a great deal of money today, but in 1928 it was everything we had. Daddy claimed the house wasn't his, it belonged to his daughters, but he handed over all his savings and insurance, every cent he had accumulated in a lifetime of hard work, and declared bankruptcy. The Ericksons were not satisfied.

They sued again, claiming that Daddy's deeding of the house to his daughters for a dollar was "fraudulent, designed to delay and defraud his creditors." Again the Ericksons won, and again the sheriff appeared, this time to foreclose on the house and to arrest Daddy and take him off to jail.

This whole affair gave me the most distorted view of justice and so-called due process. To my mind, Daddy was blameless. The judge must have thought so too, because he released Daddy from jail almost immediately, but said that he must remain within the city limits of Mayville for a year. Mayville was about twenty miles from Celoron, so DeDe had to board him out with some farm relatives for the year.

But Daddy's ruin was still incomplete. In September 1928, our beloved little house in Celoron was put on the auction block. Curiosity-seekers came tramping over Daddy's vegetable garden and poking into the chicken coop, and charging up and down the stairs and opening closet doors. To me, it was the final straw—the most unjust, inhuman thing I had ever heard of. I just couldn't understand it at all. The house was worth $4,000, but only brought $2,600 at auction. All of this was swallowed up by the mortgage Daddy still owed, and various legal fees, and so the Ericksons got nothing.

They took our house, the furnishings that DeDe had bought so laboriously on time, week after week, the insurance—everything. It was god-awful; unbelievable. My grandfather never worked again. The heart went out of him. I don't see how anyone can reconcile the punishment with the crime in this case. It made me suspicious of the law forever. And a fear of guns has stayed with me to this day.

It ruined Celoron for us; it destroyed our life together there. We moved away to a little apartment on Wilcox Avenue in Jamestown. I entered my junior year in a new, strange high school, which I hated. Shortly after this, I began running away. I'd take off to Chicago, Cleveland, Buffalo, anywhere. I bought my first dog, a little fox terrier, and named him Whooppee. Wherever I went, Whooppee went too, but sometimes my driving was too much for him. Once I hit eighty-eight miles an hour on one of the local dirt roads, and Whooppee jumped right out of the car and broke a leg.

I itched to go places and do things. DeDe was beside herself with worry about me. She finally decided that if I was bound to run away, it would be better if she helped and guided me. So one night at dinner in our little Wilcox Avenue apartment, she said to me, "Lucille, how would you like to go to dramatic school?"

My eyes popped. "Could we afford it?"

"I've already been to the bank, and they'll lend me the money," DeDe told me. My mother was always willing to go into hock for a good cause.

Modeling days,
New York,
circa 1930.

Chapter
3
♥

ctors and actresses all strive for affection. We get up on a stage because we want to be loved. The stage fulfills this need better than anything else; especially if you've found a rapport with an audience and can wrap them up in your arms and hug them close.

The irony is that in our terrible need to be loved, we pick an arena where we can also be rejected by the greatest possible number of people. Nothing's quite so wonderful as those waves of love and applause splashing over the footlights—and nothing quite as shattering as when an audience doesn't like you. All you've got to sell is yourself; rejection can't be anything but highly personal.

I didn't begin to have what it takes to succeed in show business when I first came to New York City as an upstate country kid of seventeen. DeDe and I chose the John Murray Anderson–Robert Milton theater school in New York mainly because the tuition was a bit cheaper than in other dramatic schools. To save more money, I lived with some elderly friends of the family on Dyckman Street in upper Manhattan.

The day I left, Johnny drove me to Buffalo, some seventy miles from home. From there, I took the New York Central south. New York City scared me to death and still does. It has something to do with all that cold concrete and steel instead of grass and trees. I was terrified and struck dumb by everyone at the dramatic school.

Robert Milton, one of the heads of the school, was my elocution teacher. The very first day, he asked me to pronounce "horses" and "water." The class giggled as I complied, and Mr. Milton struck his brow in exaggerated horror. "How *midwestern!*" he remarked. "We'll have to change *that!*" I could tell right off he wasn't too fond of me.

In short order they discovered that I couldn't sing, I couldn't dance, I couldn't control my body or my voice properly. Both students and teachers ignored me, which almost seemed fitting. To me, everyone was head and shoulders above me in every way.

Another student at the school earned raves for everything she did. A short, dynamic blonde, she projected with great verve. Bette Davis went on to confirm the school's belief in her awe-inspiring abilities.

At the end of the term, the school wrote my mother and said they were sorry but I didn't have what it takes to be an actress. She would be "wasting her money" if I continued. Of the seventy students who began that term, only twelve made it; I was one of the failures.

Although lonely, homesick, and lost, I couldn't face the sneers and snickers I felt would be waiting for me back in Jamestown. This was the day of the Ziegfeld Follies and Shubert spectacles; hundreds of girls were hired to decorate the stage in fur and feathers. So I decided to become a showgirl.

I soon learned that to survive in the theater you have to be very strong, very healthy, and damned resilient. Rarely does anyone give you an encouraging word. And I dreaded that inevitable question, "Do you have any Broadway experience?"

I'd stick out my thin chest and say brightly, "No, sir, I haven't done anything on Broadway, but I'd sure like to try." I'd then add that I'd come all the way from Butte, Montana. This eager and slightly dishonest little speech won me five jobs in various musicals, such as rear-line chorus girl in the third road company of *Rio Rita*. No one got paid for rehearsals in those days, so DeDe dug deep to keep me afloat.

One morning, I woke up to find that all I had was four pennies. Subway fare to the theater district was a nickel. So I panhandled for a penny. One well-dressed older man stopped to listen, then offered me a ten-dollar bill. "Listen, mister," I told him with a withering look, "all I want is *one* penny." He's probably still standing there with his mouth open!

LUCILLE BALL

The seductive Shubert girls were mean old harpies. They hated all competition, especially seventeen-year-old kids. I'd show up early for rehearsals and stay until they had to sweep me off the stage with the cigar butts, but I couldn't seem to get the hang of things, even if all I had to do was walk. I was supposed to project sultry sex, but all I managed to get across was my awkward timidity.

I was so shy that all I could do was shrink in a corner and watch and listen. If someone asked me a question, words stuck in my throat. Time after time, I'd rehearse for several weeks and then get fired. I was never around long enough for the first costume fitting. I don't blame the directors. I'd have fired that cringing scaredy-cat Lucille Ball too.

But I didn't give up. I wore out my soles trudging to casting offices and stuffed the holes with newspaper. I lurked behind coffee bars waiting for customers to leave. In 1928, you got two doughnuts and a cup of coffee for a dime. Often a customer might leave one doughnut uneaten and a nickel tip. I'd wiggle into his seat fast, devour the leftover doughnut, and order coffee with the tip.

Then I was picked for the chorus of a Fred and Paula Stone show; it was *Stepping Stones.* When five weeks had passed and I was still with the show, my spirits skyrocketed. Then late one night the producer called for some revisions in the dance numbers. Around midnight, the director finally said, "We're going to add some ballet, girls. Anybody who can't do toe work is out of the show."

To me he added, "Forget it, Two-Gun. You're a nice

kid but you just don't have it. Why don't you go home to Montana and raise a big family?"

I dug my hands into my empty pockets and trudged the long blocks north to my fleabag apartment in a Columbus Circle rooming house. I can't say that I was discouraged. For some incomprehensible reason, I knew that someday I'd make it as an actress. I just decided to postpone the struggle for a while. I didn't want to be a drag on DeDe any longer.

Here's what I advise any young struggling actress today: The important thing is to develop as a woman first, and a performer second. You wouldn't prostitute yourself to get a part, not if you're in your right mind. You won't be happy, whatever you do, unless you're comfortable with your own conscience. Keep your head up, keep your shoulders back, keep your self-respect, be nice, be smart. And remember that there are practically no "overnight" successes. Before that brilliant hit performance came ten, fifteen, sometimes twenty years in the salt mines, sweating it out.

I cured myself of my shyness when it finally occurred to me that people didn't think about me nearly as much as I gave them credit for. The truth was, nobody really gave a damn. Like most teenagers, I was much too self-centered. When I stopped being prisoner to what I worried was others' opinions of me, I became more confident and free. But I still needed to eat.

It was midnight on a Saturday when I was fired from *Stepping Stones* after five weeks of rehearsals—with no pay. Sunday I leafed through the classified ads, and early Monday morning I landed a twenty-five-dollar-a-week job modeling coats. A steady diet of coffee and doughnuts hadn't added much flesh to my figure, so I decided that winter coats would hide my skinniness.

My fellow models were a helpful bunch. They got me blind dates for dinner and taught me how to stretch that dinner into two.

I watched in admiration as a redheaded model gave me my first lesson. With a wink at me, while the waiter wasn't watching, she first put a linen table napkin into her handbag, then several buttered rolls, celery and olives, and a big slice of roast beef. Sometimes if you brought a big enough bag you could squeeze in a little French pastry, too.

My first modeling job was a good one in a small wholesale coat place on Seventh Avenue run by some nice elderly Jewish people. Then I worked at a dress-and-suit house, where I told them my name was Diane Belmont. I had always liked the name Diane; Belmont racetrack on Long Island inspired the last name. Some of my old friends on Seventh Avenue still call me Diane. They think Hollywood changed my name to Lucille Ball.

All the time I was in New York I was sick with longing for my family. When I couldn't stand it any longer, I'd pack up and go home for a while. Back home I worked as a clerk in a dress shop and as a Walgreen's soda jerk across from the Jamestown Hotel. Daddy was still staying with relatives in Mayville, and once in a while we'd borrow a car and take him out for a drive. I remember how we'd panic if we accidentally

drove outside the Mayville city limits, since he was still prohibited from leaving.

Daddy was in a highly depressed state of mind, and I
worried about him constantly. One day, toward the end of his
year's sentence, I heard that our farm relatives picked strawberries, and that that was all they were giving Daddy to eat.
Just strawberries, three times a day. My good friend Marion
Strong remembers that I was so upset, and so furious, I threw
a tantrum unlike any before. I threw plates and pillows,
stomped my feet, roared, then wept. She was afraid I'd lost my
sanity. "I'll make it up to Daddy someday!" I vowed loudly.
"I'll show 'em, you'll see!"

How I was going to do this, I had no idea. But I knew
I couldn't do it as a soda jerk in Jamestown. So back to New
York I went, and this time my luck improved. I moved into an
atmosphere of gilded elegance. I became a model at Hattie
Carnegie's internationally famous dress shop on East Forty-
ninth Street. Overnight, I found myself in a world of rich society women, glamorous movie stars, and free-spending
men-about-town.

Hattie was born Henrietta Kanengeiser, the daughter
of a Viennese immigrant who settled in Manhattan's Lower
East Side. When Hattie opened her first shop, on Tenth Street,
she took the name Carnegie in tribute to one of America's
greatest success stories. Her partner, Rosie Roth, whom I got
to know very well, designed dresses and Hattie made hats.

Hattie combined unerring good taste and a shrewd
business sense; her shop was a fabulous success right from the

start, and she and Rosie moved uptown, nearer the carriage trade. Just a few years before I first went to New York, Hattie bought a brownstone at 42 East Forty-ninth Street. Her salon was lavishly beautiful, with entire rooms of gold-leaf antiques from French châteaux. Hattie was a tiny dynamo, direct and outspoken. She wouldn't let anyone buy a dress she considered unbecoming. Gertrude Lawrence once spent $22,000 in a single afternoon in her shop. I'm told she would have spent more, but Hattie didn't approve of some of her choices.

Hattie taught me how to slouch properly in a $1,000 hand-sewn sequin dress and how to wear a $40,000 sable coat as casually as rabbit. Since I was her youngest and least experienced model, I was soon covered with bruises where she kicked me in the shins to remind me to bend my knees properly, or pinched me in the ribs to make me raise my chest higher. Fiery, volatile Hattie fired me at least once a week, but like all the other models, I responded not to those outbursts but to her great warmth, and loved her.

Mostly I modeled long, slinky evening gowns and suits, thirty to forty changes a day. With each change I had to slip into matching shoes, whether they were my size or not, and go wobbling out over the ultrathick carpet. By nighttime my feet were as swollen and sore as my shins. For this I earned the princely sum of thirty-five dollars a week, good wages back in 1929.

Connie and Joan Bennett were frequent customers and I lost no time in bleaching my hair the color of Joan's and imitating her style: flat on top with dippy waves on each side.

Joan Crawford, Gloria Swanson, and Ina Claire also came to Hattie's. I tried to analyze their styles: how they walked and moved their hands and eyes, what they wore, and how they talked. I also scrutinized the Social Register, full of Vanderbilts and Whitneys and Rhinelanders to whom a price tag was just something a maid snipped off a dress. Barbara Hutton bought carloads of clothes. And at the Plaza and St. Regis and Pierre hotels, where we appeared in all the important fashion shows, I learned to recognize all the leading debutantes.

I didn't know it at the time, but I was storing up a lot of useful knowledge. An actress must draw upon her own background; what she has lived, seen, and observed. It's often been pointed out that Ginger Rogers and I can function on any level: high society, middle-class, and street urchin. A superb comedienne like Irene Dunne was only convincing in well-bred parts. Ginger could play a finishing-school girl, a housewife, or Kitty Foyle. I can be as regal as a marquise, if the part calls for it, or peel a potato convincingly.

By the time I worked for Hattie, I was no longer Diane Belmont, but Lucille Ball. I can't say that I enjoyed the life of a high-fashion model; I hated the stagnation that sets in when you are just a clotheshorse. At Hattie's I felt like a well-dressed dummy. But I did get out and see things and meet people for the first time in my life. And some pretty funny things could happen. I remember one time I wore a very tight-fitting Paris import to a horse show at Belmont; all of Long Island society was there, and we models were driven about in a Pierce-Arrow touring car to show off our clothes. My dress was organza, with a hand-painted fish-scale design all over it. A sudden thundershower drenched us, and the fish scales were applied to my skin—all over. I thought I'd be a mermaid permanently.

As a Hattie Carnegie model, I began meeting some of the rich eligible bachelors in town, like Sailing Baruch, Jr., Pat di Cicco, and Cubby Broccoli. Nightlife in New York then was a wonderful spree. You could dance until dawn in Harlem, watch the sun come up over Central Park, and breakfast in Greenwich Village. There were hundreds of supper shows and nightclubs, and an endless number of big Broadway openings.

I had the usual proposals, but at eighteen, marriage was the last thing on my mind. I feel sorry for young people today who feel so alone that they have to mate with their first crush. It shocks me that so many young brides are pregnant at the altar. When you have kids late in life, you appreciate them more. They keep you young, and you see the world through better eyes. You can give your children a finer sense of values, too, because if you're lucky, your own values have improved with time.

But like today's teenagers, I got little sleep and seldom ate the kind of food my body needed. One winter day, I came down with a bad cold that turned into pneumonia. I stayed in my room restlessly for several days, tossing with fever, but then hurried back to Hattie's. I needed that thirty-five dollars a week.

I was standing on the dais for a fitting when suddenly I felt as if both my legs were on fire. The pain was excruciating. Hattie kindly sent me to her own doctor, around the corner on Fifth Avenue. He told me that the pains were arthritic, possibly rheumatoid arthritis. This is an incurable disease which becomes progressively more crippling until the sufferer ends up in a wheelchair for life.

"You must go to a hospital at once," Hattie's doctor told me.

I did some rapid calculations. "I only have eighty-five dollars to my name," I told him.

He then gave me the address of an orthopedic clinic up near Columbia University. That night I sat waiting my turn for three hours while the city's poor, some of them horribly crippled, went in and out. It was ten o'clock before my turn came.

The clinic doctor examined me and shook his head. I was by this time crying and half fainting from the pain. He asked if he could try a new and radical treatment, some kind of horse serum, and I said yes, for God's sake, anything. For several weeks I stayed in my room, and he came and gave me injections; finally, when my money ran out and my legs still were not better, there was nothing left to do but go home to Jamestown. One of my beaux drove me to Grand Central Station and pushed me to the train in a wheelchair. I was discouraged but not terribly frightened. The confidence of the young is truly remarkable.

Johnny met my train at Buffalo and drove me to my

family's apartment on Wilcox Avenue. Daddy was back home again, thank goodness. He lectured me on taking better care of myself, and DeDe, although still working all day long herself, devoted her evenings to massaging my legs and cheering me up.

For the first few months I was in such pain that time passed in a kind of blur. We kept up the horse serum injections, which were then considered a highly experimental, even last-ditch experiment. I was a guinea pig who survived, and the pain gradually subsided. Finally the day came when, with the support of Daddy and the doctor, I shakily stood up. We found that my left leg was now somewhat shorter than my right leg.

It also pulled sideways, and to correct this, I wore a twenty-pound weight in one of my ugly black orthopedic shoes. The metal weight felt cold against my foot, and the pain as I clomped around was like needles. For my morale, I wore some heavy blue satin pajamas that I had bought on sale at Hattie's. Pajamas for women were just becoming fashionable; I think I was also the first female in Jamestown to appear on the street in slacks.

One happy result of my long illness was that I did learn to take better care of myself. I tried to get my full eight hours' sleep a night, and I ate fewer starches and carbohydrates. I still go without the right food when I'm busy, and often skip lunch or dinner altogether. This has the strange effect of making me gain weight, since my body retains fluid. Dr. Henry Beiler, whose patients include Greta Garbo and Gloria Swanson,

wants me to eat a small meal every few hours, and I'm trying
to do this. He doesn't believe in pills or medicines, but he ac-
complishes wonders with food. It's shocking how many doctors in Beverly Hills never once ask during a consultation
what you eat.

In the late spring of 1930, I was still convalescing at
home, my legs thin as matchsticks, when Bill Bemus came to
see me. Bill had been a professional actor on Broadway and
so the Jamestown Players had asked him to produce and direct a fast-paced melodrama called *Within the Law*. Bill had seen
me in various amateur productions around town since he'd first
been impressed by my work in *The Scottish Rite Revue*. He had
a difficult part to cast in his new play: an ingenue who could
convincingly play a cheap gangster's moll and also a debutante.
Back in 1930, debutantes were considered models of good
manners and breeding.

Bill looked at me with my bright bleached hair, blue
satin pajamas, and blood-red fingernails and burst out, "You
are Aggie Lynch. Will you play the part?"

"Who's Aggie Lynch?" I wanted to know. He then described to me the big scene of the play.

Aggie is a hard-boiled confidence woman who black-
mails married men. But when she's pinched and taken to the
precinct station, she convinces the police inspector that he's
made a bad mistake. She isn't the notorious Aggie at all, but
the debutante daughter of the richest banker in town. The terribly cultured Aggie is highly insulted at being brought in like
a common criminal.

The inspector apologizes humbly. But just as she's about to sweep haughtily out, a cop enters and greets her casually, "Hello, Aggie."

Her real identity uncovered, Aggie reverts to her real self. "So you think I'll squeal," she sneers, coming back to the police inspector's desk. "Sure I'll squeal—like *hell!*"

Well, that was pretty sensational in 1930, hearing a young girl come out with *that*. Gasps of horror, twitters, snickers; we really got 'em. It was funny to think how tongue-tied and awkward I'd been in dramatic school; here in my beloved Jamestown I didn't have a shred of self-consciousness. Bill Bemus told me I exuded personality. "You're better than the original Aggie on Broadway," he told me. "You can do tragedy, comedy, anything." Then the crowning glory: "You're a *professional.*"

The *Jamestown Journal* called me "sensational, another Jeanne Eagels." Eagels, of course, played the prostitute in Somerset Maugham's *Rain*.

We took the play to the Chautauqua Institute and gave another highly successful performance there. My friend Marion Strong couldn't get over how naturally I took to the stage. My poise was unshaken, even when a mouse ran across the stage in the middle of one of my big soliloquies. For the part of Aggie I dyed my hair dark, and just before the performance, Marion tinted it with "golden glint," which gave it a reddish cast. For the first time I began to wonder if maybe I didn't have a redheaded personality. But Broadway seemed as far off as ever.

In the summer of 1930 another tragedy befell our family. Aunt Lola had completed her nurse's training and was then head of a psychiatric ward in a mental hospital in Long Island. Apparently, she had been bothered by stomach pains for some time, which she foolishly ignored; one night a patient kicked her in the stomach and she died that night of peritonitis. Almost immediately, Uncle George Mandicos appeared and took Cleo away with him to Buffalo.

My little cousin was only eleven when overnight she found herself in a motherless home, with a father she hardly knew, in a Greek community where everything was strange to her: the food, the customs, the language. It just about broke her heart, and DeDe's too. The double loss of Lola and Cleo severely upset us all.

A few weeks after Cleo left, the pier ballroom at Celoron Amusement Park burned up in a spectacular blaze on a Sunday morning. Marion Strong and I had been dancing there the night before with our dates; we wondered whose carelessly dropped cigarettes had started the fire.

Marion and I stood by the lakeshore watching the towering flames devour the old ballroom. Steam billowed up from the cold lake as the burning timbers crashed down; the dense black smoke billowing into the summer sky could be seen for miles.

This was where I'd gone to my first dance, in my pussy willow taffeta dress with its band of real fur. This was where my first bittersweet crushes were born and died to the strains of "Margie" and " 'S Wonderful" I began to cry, and then I couldn't stop.

All the ghosts in those crackling flames shooting into

the sky. My wonderful, happy childhood in Celoron gone forever, and so tragically. My first picnics in the park, what exciting occasions they were, with Flora Belle in her Sunday best, the hamper full of goodies over her arm . . . and Grandfather Fred, so good-looking with his jaunty air, his straw boater cocked over his smiling blue eyes. And Lola, with her sunny ways, honeymooning with George, and Cleo, with her dimples. Marion was crying too, and we clung together, drowning in a sea of tears. Marion says that she never cried so much again in her whole life; I wish I could say the same.

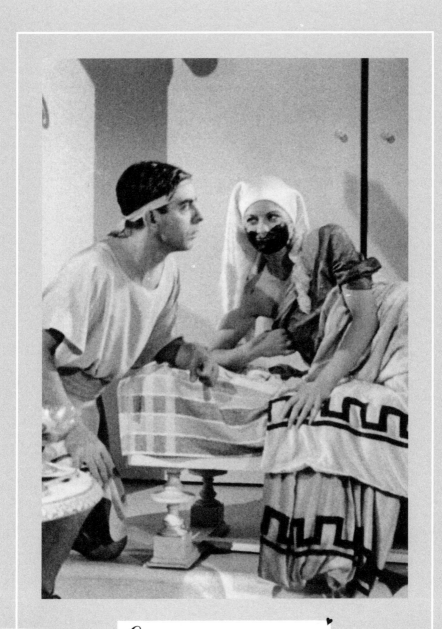

*E*ddie Cantor commended Lucille
for putting comedy first despite
the risk to her glamour,
a rule that she followed
throughout her career.

C h a p t e r
4
♥

*I*t was the following spring that I persuaded Marion to go with me to New York to look for work. We each had twenty dollars in our handbags the day a friend drove us to the city. I knew enough free-lance illustrators to earn forty dollars a week posing for coffee and cigarette ads; Marion found a job in a Greenwich Village antique shop. At the Hotel Kimberly at Broadway and Seventy-fourth Street, we shared a room with twin beds and bath for eighteen dollars a week. We even shared one bureau.

Marion had a lot of stubborn Swede in her; I tried to organize her life too much, she complained. I felt protective toward her, but when I gave her too much advice, she got mad. We had some lulus of fights. Once I didn't approve of some guy she was seeing and we argued half the night. The next morning, as I was hurrying to get ready for work, I remembered that it was Marion's twentieth birthday. I ran out, bought some fresh spring daffodils, and jammed them into a water glass on the bureau. "Happy birthday, old scrap iron!" I scrawled on a note while she slept. Marion, bless her, still treasures that note.

Marion was timid about many things. I could never talk her into traveling underground on the subway. When we walked about New York, I ran at full tilt, dodging between people on the sidewalks. I seldom waited for a light to change, but was halfway across on the red while Marion quivered on the corner.

She got homesick for Jamestown after a few months and went back home; in a couple of years she was married and raising a family. I got a job modeling in a first-class clothing house owned by a wonderful couple named Jackson. Hattie Carnegie's mink-lined establishment made me uncomfortable, but the Jacksons' was a fun place, full of warmth and laughter and a family feeling. The clothes were exquisite and expensive, but instead of bored socialites for customers, we had women department store buyers, full of talk and gossip, sharp as foxes.

I clowned around a lot and made them laugh; this didn't hurt sales any. At that time, I lived in an East Side flat directly over an Italian restaurant reeking of garlic. I gave the buyers a demonstration of how I went stamping and banging and singing up the stairs when I got home at night to chase the rats and cockroaches away.

The designer was Rosie Roth, who had been Hattie Carnegie's partner at the start of her meteoric career. The Jacksons paid her $25,000 a year—an unheard-of salary for a woman designer then—and sent her to Paris several times a year. Rosie brought back trunkloads of French silks and satins heavy enough to stand alone. Her creations were fitted individually to seven models; often I stood for three hours or so while she draped and tucked and pleated, her mouth full of pins. When I got bored, I'd camp—that's a show business word for getting playful.

"This girl's fullahell," Rosie would complain, sticking me with a pin to make me behave. "You got flair, you got personality, a beautiful body you got," she told me. "So why so aggravating? You make my ulcer ache."

Sometimes she'd yell, "You're fired!" I'd run out of the place gleefully, knowing that a phone call that evening would rehire me.

This was in the days before air-conditioning, and dresses weren't lined. When the temperature stood at 100 in that stuffy little fitting room, the black fuzz from the long velvet gowns would stick to our bodies in the heat and stuff our pores. Whew! I can still feel it now.

No matter: I was happy there because the Jacksons treated their models like their own daughters. When I had dinner dates with nice young men, Mrs. Jackson often let me borrow one of Rosie's glittering creations. Of course, I had to get it back early in the morning, before Rosie arrived for work. She objected to the models parading her originals around town, getting cigarette burns and gravy stains on them, but the Jacksons were most generous and understanding.

I was the "bride" who ended every fashion show. The tired dress buyers with their aching varicose veins would drop in just to see me whirl around in yards of white lace or organdy or satin. Some girls are perennial bridesmaids; I was the perennial bride: platinum-blond and blue-eyed, full of naive girlish dreams. And, as Rosie was always telling me, fullahell.

A movie scout saw me one night at a Silk Ball. He telephoned me the next day at work to suggest a movie test. This was the beginning of July, our busiest season, so I told him over the phone, "Well, thanks very much, but I couldn't possibly. . . . All the buyers are in town and we're showing our new line. . . . My outfits are made just for me, and nobody else can model them."

I hung up and dismissed the whole thing from my mind. But my boss, Mr. Jackson, had overheard the conversation. He made me phone back.

"Paramount wants to test me every day this week!" I told him.

"Wonderful!" replied Mr. Jackson. "That's more important than modeling a few clothes. Say you'll go."

That bighearted, wonderful man insisted that I take the tests, but they came to nothing. I still wasn't photogenic, it seemed.

I continued working at the Jacksons', and during these Depression years, DeDe separated from Ed. This upheaval, along with losing Cleo, gave her a bad time emotionally, so I suggested that she send Freddy to New York to live with me. He came and shared my dark little apartment over the Italian restaurant, and went to high school in New York until DeDe's health improved. When she recovered her spirits, we all got an apartment together: me, DeDe, Daddy, and Freddy. My mother found a job as a saleslady at Stern's on Forty-second Street. At night our bathroom looked like a Chinese laundry—Daddy even washed his own shirts—but at last we were together.

For Daddy, however, the move was a catastrophe. He was already in his late sixties. Too old to find a job during the Depression, he had nothing to do but brood alone in the apartment or walk the city streets. The filth and misery of New York City slums was worse than anything he had ever seen or imagined. He began to worry about the world and everyone in it.

To earn more money, I often posed at night and weekends for commercial illustrators. A free-lance painter named Ratterman did an oil portrait of me in a flowing chiffon dress— something I'd borrowed overnight from Rosie. Later he added two gray Russian wolfhounds for a touch of class. To my great surprise, he sold the painting to Chesterfield cigarettes and overnight my face and figure were on billboards all over town. Russell Markert, director of the Rockettes at Radio City Music Hall, noticed the new Chesterfield Girl high over Times Square and recognized me. He'd met me briefly back in my days with Hattie. Sylvia Hahlo, a theatrical agent, noticed me too. She had her eyes open for young models who might profitably be exported to Hollywood, and she knew my face and name from many fashion shows.

The Jacksons' wholesale house was at Thirty-ninth Street and Seventh Avenue; often on my lunch hour I'd walk the few blocks to Times Square and gaze wistfully at the photographs in the theater lobbies. One humid July day I was browsing in front of the Palace Theater, when I heard a woman's voice at my elbow.

"Lucille Ball! Just the person I was looking for. How would you like to go to Hollywood?"

I turned and saw Sylvia Hahlo. "Who? Er . . . ah . . . what?"

"You're the latest Chesterfield Girl, aren't you?" Sylvia continued. "Well, Sam Goldwyn, the producer, needs a dozen well-known poster girls for a new Eddie Cantor movie, *Roman Scandals.* He had twelve all picked, but one just backed out, and they're scheduled to leave for Hollywood in three days and—"

"Who do I see?" I interrupted. "Where do I go?"

Sylvia nodded over my shoulder. "Right up those stairs by the Palace Theater. Second floor. Jim Mulvey—he's Mr. Goldwyn's New York agent."

"Thanks," I yelled over my shoulder, in a dead run.

"Don't forget my ten percent," Sylvia called after me.

This was on a Wednesday. Fortunately, there was no time for a screen test, or I might never have been accepted. Jim

Mulvey liked my enthusiasm and signed me on the spot. I had a guarantee of $125 a week for six weeks, plus free transportation. The Jacksons gave me a leave of absence with their blessings—even though it just about ruined their fall show. So on Saturday, just three days after my fateful brush with Sylvia Hahlo, DeDe and Daddy saw me off on the Super Chief for Hollywood.

Everything happened so fast that I had no chance to realize that this was my first major break, a marvelous stroke of good luck. And of course, I expected to be back in New York before the maple leaves flamed in Central Park.

DeDe had a story she used to tell us about Hollywood when we were small that we loved hearing over and over. When she went out there following the death of my father, Douglas Fairbanks and Mary Pickford were America's sweethearts. DeDe had the good fortune to be on the same train with Mr. Fairbanks. As it drew into Los Angeles, the acrobatic actor jumped from the train and vaulted a low barrier by the tracks into the arms of the golden Miss Pickford, who was waiting for him in a baby-blue convertible. Here were all the ingredients of the Hollywood Dream: sex, glamour, money, a handsome young couple, adored by millions and adoring each other.

In my wildest dreams, I never expected to get to Hollywood, yet here I was, riding into the same station I'd heard DeDe describe so often, with a movie contract in my pocketbook, already creased with wrinkles from having been read so often.

Hollywood in 1933 was a busy, bustling place, full of men-about-town and producers chasing would-be starlets around that famous piece of furniture, the casting couch. But not Lucy. I was one of the lucky few to arrive in movieland with a contract. I was already under a studio's protective wing. In those days that was a blessed way to begin.

There was a big hoopla when we arrived at the Pasadena station, with a crush of photographers, press agents, and studio people. I was wearing a black silk dress with a demure white collar, an outfit Constance Bennett made famous. The Hattie Carnegie dress was five years old, but I felt like a queen in it.

We drove from Pasadena to Hollywood. Hollywood looked like a sleepy little village completely ringed by hills, a place of wondrous beauty after the dirt and grime of New York.

I just sat back in my cushioned limousine seat and drank it all in: the olive and lemon and orange trees, the strange and exotic flowers, the chorus of birds. And over everything, the clearest, purest air . . . You felt you could reach out and touch a mountain twenty miles away. Nobody thought of smog in those days; like TV, it didn't exist.

We were taken to the Roosevelt Hotel for my first press interview, where I was dumb enough to tell reporters my right age: twenty-one. We met Sam Goldwyn and other studio executives, who asked us where we wanted to live. I decided on a one-room Murphy-bed apartment on Formosa Street, about three blocks from the United Artists studio where *Roman Scandals* was to be filmed.

Finally it was time to report for work. I try to learn from past experiences, and my miserable failure as a dramatic student still rankled. I vowed that I wasn't going to muff this unique opportunity by being tongue-tied and stiff and self-conscious. By this time, too—after my happy years at the Jacksons' modeling—I liked myself better.

The next morning at the studio we were handed skimpy jersey bathing suits and told to line up. Chiefly, that's what we did—for months: line up and wait. I weighed only 111 pounds and the other girls were sort of voluptuous, so while we waited, I padded myself with gloves or paper or old banana peels, anything I could find just to make fun.

When Eddie Cantor walked down the line to give each Goldwyn Girl the once-over, I made a special effort. I remembered a trick I'd seen Dorothy Gish do at Belmont racetrack. She and her sister Lillian were sitting in a box with two gentlemen when the Hattie Carnegie models were ushered into seats right behind them. After a while, Lillian went off with the gentlemen. Dorothy was just sitting there, tearing off little pieces of paper from her bright red program. Then she turned around, and I saw that she had stuck them like measles spots all over her face. Well, I thought this was about the funniest thing I'd ever seen. So as Eddie Cantor started down the line, I tore up some little pieces of red crepe paper, wet them with my tongue, and stuck them all over my bare arms and chest and face. When Mr. Cantor got to me, his jaw dropped, his big eyes popped, and then he roared with laughter. He asked me my name. He told everyone about "that Ball dame— she's a riot." I was in heaven.

Roman Scandals was one of United Artists' biggest musical extravaganzas of 1933. The Depression hit Hollywood hard at first, but since movie tickets cost only fifty cents, the movie industry suffered less than the Broadway theater. By 1933 people were happy to plunk down half a dollar to forget temporarily the grim bread lines and bank closings.

In addition to Eddie Cantor, *Roman Scandals* had Ruth Etting, Gloria Stuart, Alan Mowbray, and Edward Arnold. Cantor was the emperor's food taster in the times of the Roman Empire. The fresh and funny script was written by George Kaufman and Robert Sherwood; the songs included the tuneful "Keep Young and Beautiful" and "Build a Little Home." According to one reviewer, *Roman Scandals* was "photographed lavishly and set with considerable taste. Eddie is surrounded by beautiful girls who seem in their languid splendor to have stepped out of a frame devised by the late Florenz Ziegfeld."

Languid may have been how we appeared; exhaustion was the cause. They used very large sets with tremendous casts and many, many klieg lights. And this was in July. The lights were terribly dangerous in those days and detrimental to your eyes. When the director yelled, "Okay, hit the lights!" everyone knew it was time to look down. If you looked directly at the lights, you got a piercing, knifelike pain in your head; so you looked at the floor until your eyes got adjusted. Even so, we Goldwyn Girls all went to bed with raw potato poultices on our eyes, those klieg lights burned our eyeballs so.

In one particular scene we slave girls were high up in a rotunda, chained by our wrists, in the nude supposedly, while the slave traders with long black whips walked around below, picking out the girls they wanted. We wore long hemp wigs, which came to our knees, with a few scraps of chiffon underneath.

In those days there were no definite working hours. We slaved all day, and sometimes until three in the morning. We'd come to the studio at six a.m., get body makeup on, and then get chained up in the rotunda. Shooting didn't always start right away, and they didn't get you down between shots because that was too much trouble. One particular time, they had left us up there several hours and some of us weren't feeling too well . . . this had been going on for weeks. Suddenly I fainted and fell. The fake chains holding my wrists gave way and I started to fall toward those bare burning klieg lights below. There was a scramble and one of the slave drivers, Dewey Robinson, a big, bulky, wonderful man, caught me just before I hit those sizzling lamps. It scared the hell out of me, but otherwise I was fine.

Yet as rough as the hours and conditions were, the food was terrific. For the emperor's banquet scenes, a catering service wheeled into the studio whole hot roasted pigs, barbecued baby lamb, sides of juicy beef, and mountains of fruit and pastry. It was the most delicious food I'd ever tasted in my entire life. I especially enjoyed the "ostrich eggs." These were real ostrich eggshells filled with rich, creamy custard. Maybe I was just hungry for real food after all those doughnuts; I gobbled that stuff up day after day while the camera ground and the lights frizzled my rope wig, until I became horribly sick to my stomach. It was years before I could touch custard again.

One of the worst things the studio people did was

shave off my eyebrows. We were all trying to look like Jean Harlow. Now God forbid that I should ever find myself on a desert island without an eyebrow pencil. It's the first thing I reach for every morning. The only girl I know who managed to grow hers back again was Ginger Rogers, and even then it took her years.

Roman Scandals was supposed to be filmed in six weeks, but it stretched into six months. I loved everything about moviemaking: the money, meeting so many different kinds of people, the high excitement of each day, the fantastic talent of the technicians who could put the Colosseum on a thirty-foot stage. But my movie career might have ended there, and I'd have been a fifty-dollar-a-week model in New York again, except for another remarkable stroke of good luck.

One day a light, graceful young man came on the set and called to me, "Hello, Lucille!" Then he introduced himself as Russell Markert and reminded me that we had already met in New York. He was going to be the choreographer for a big film, *Moulin Rouge*, starring Constance Bennett and Franchot Tone. Russell was visiting the *Roman Scandals* set to see if he could pick some showgirls for his film. Now, I've got long legs and a *sense* of rhythm, but a tin ear when it comes to distinguishing musical measures. Russell knew I'd never be a Ruby Keeler, but he said he could teach me what was required. And so, just as *Roman Scandals* was through, the Goldwyn Girls were loaned out en masse to Darryl Zanuck at 20th Century–Fox.

That's the way it worked back then. Sometimes I'd be

loaned out and I didn't even know what the movie was about or who was in it. I wouldn't even know the title. I'd just show up at the studio at a certain hour, walk through a scene, maybe say one line. I never knew I was in *Broadway Through a Keyhole* with Russ Columbo until a few weeks ago, when I saw the film for the first time.

Life was hectic but the money was good. I thought I was doing great until Russell Markert impressed upon me the necessity of saving. You don't have to start a savings account with a thousand dollars, he used to tell me. You can start with one dollar. On his advice, I put twenty-five dollars into the bank every payday. Otherwise, he said, I would never survive the parched periods between pictures. By this time, I was determined to stay in Hollywood. I would do what I could to make sure I'd survive the long haul.

Under Russell Markert's prodding, I bought a bicycle to save taxi fare. I enjoyed pedaling through the rosy dawn, past the little white bungalows, each with its garden of pink camellias and purple bougainvillea. I pictured my poor family back in New York City in their grimy walk-up flat and pictured myself, too, back in the modeling business.

I worked long, hard hours without complaint, but some nights after hours of dance rehearsals my legs would really ache. One evening as Russell was walking along Hollywood Boulevard, a yellow cab shot past him with a familiar-looking green bicycle on the running board. He then recognized me at the wheel and the cabbie in the backseat with a disgruntled expression, both arms out the window hanging on to the bicycle. After a sixteen-hour day, I found that the bike ride home was just too much.

One of my few extravagances was to telephone DeDe in New York. I'd say hello and then start to bawl. After three minutes of this, DeDe would start worrying about the charges and she'd hang up. I told them they were all coming to Hollywood just as soon as I'd saved up their fares. And that week I'd try very hard to save an extra five or ten dollars.

It was in Hollywood that I finally got Johnny out of my system. The reason was another older man, a handsome, sophisticated matinee idol of the London and New York stage. Ralph Forbes was about thirty and had just been divorced from Ruth Chatterton. He could play Ibsen or Noël Coward. He was terribly British, and so was his whole family; they impressed the hell out of me. But when he proposed, I cooled off in a hurry. I just couldn't picture myself in his rarefied British atmosphere. I'm not the crooked-finger-and-teacup type. Ralph had wealth, fame, talent, looks—why would he need me? I was more than half in love with him, but I managed to turn him down. Almost immediately he eloped to Yuma with a young British actress, Heather Angel, and that abrupt switch convinced me that I had made the right decision.

I decided to forget about romance and to concentrate on my career. In rapid succession I had brief walk-on parts in *Murder at the Vanities*, *Bottoms Up*, and *Affairs of Cellini*. While making one Goldwyn picture I had a cough, and as we did our dance routine I kept hacking. Finally, Busby Berkeley glowered at me and said, *"Please!"* and I said, "I'm sorry, but I can't help it." I probably had a 103-degree temperature as well. Somebody handed me some cough syrup and I gulped down half the bottle, unaware of its codeine content. Then I crept into the wings and fell asleep. I slept so soundly that it was hours before they found me. Mr. Goldwyn never forgot that, because I held up production for such a long time.

After I had been in Hollywood for about a year, I went back east for a short visit. I stayed with Grandma Peterson in her narrow, dark little house in Jamestown where I had been so miserable as a child. My stepfather Ed was living with her then. He was not working and was very glad to see me; my Hollywood "success" pleased him. I told him how much his encouragement years before had meant to me.

In Hollywood, of course, I was still an unknown, but in Jamestown the newspapers made a big thing out of the premiere of *Roman Scandals*. "Jamestown's own Lucille Ball," the ads ran, with a full-length picture of me, mostly big eyes and that knee-length wig. Overnight I found myself a local celebrity.

The *Jamestown Journal* sent a reporter to interview me at Grandmother's. He asked how the twelve Goldwyn Girls were doing, and I told him that in one short year, eight had vanished. Here's what eventually happened to them: One married an English lord, another became the mistress of a Texas cattle king (and ultimately bore him four children), and a third became the lifelong mistress of another fabulously wealthy man. A fourth Goldwyn Girl of 1933 lived high and handsomely, then died of tuberculosis in the charity ward of a Hollywood hospital. Four others were happily married and raised families.

Back in Hollywood after my brief trip east, I got show-girl parts in a Bulldog Drummond film, *Nana,* and *The Bowery.* In all these pictures I was just part of the scenery, strolling past the camera in chiffon and feathers. Friends kept telling me: "You should be in comedy." I burned to get some real acting experience, so when I was offered a stock contract at Columbia, I jumped at the chance.

I took the slapstick parts the other starlets spurned, and never whined about the siphon water and pies in the face. I considered myself lucky to be paid while learning a business I adored.

We often worked past midnight. I did whatever was asked of me. My wages at Columbia were seventy-five dollars a week. Each payday I dropped into the bank across the street and added to my survival account. After Freddy graduated from high school, he came out and found a job at the Trocadero supper club. Together we rented a small furnished bungalow on Ogden Drive in Hollywood for eighty-five dollars a month and spent every spare moment fixing it up in anticipation of DeDe and Daddy's arrival.

One of the biggest stars at Columbia in those days was Ann Sothern, who was known for her extravagance and good taste. She was also loved for her generous heart. One day I got up enough courage to ask her advice about fixing up our lit-tle rented house. I was a nobody on the lot, yet she took the time to come over. She arrived in a blue Alfa Romeo with a uniformed chauffeur and dripped up the walk in a full-length mink. I was in dungarees and a bandanna scrubbing the floor. The place was a hodgepodge of patterned wallpaper, scuffed floors, and broken-down furniture. Ann raised her delicately arched eyebrows, and very kindly advised me to cover everything possible with white enamel paint, and later add ruffly white curtains and fluffy blue scatter rugs. She knew we had only pennies to spend, but thanks to her good taste, the place became fresh and sparkling, a blue and white dollhouse.

Finally, Freddy and I were ready. So excited I could hardly talk, I phoned DeDe and told her to make reservations on the Super Chief. I hung up and ten minutes later the studio called to say that I'd been fired. Columbia was giving up its stock company and we had all been laid off! Forever!

That night I had a date with a wonderful boy, Dick Green, whose brother was Johnny Green, the songwriter. "Well, I lost my job," I told him. "How do you like that? Out of the clear blue sky."

"There's a showgirl call at RKO at nine o'clock tonight," he told me. "Say, did you ever model at Bergdorf Goodman's in New York?"

When I said no, I hadn't, Dick told me, "Well, say you did, because Bernard Newman's picking the models."

The name meant nothing to me. I said okay, and went right over to RKO. They liked my height and my manner, and so I was called into the front office. Mr. Newman asked me if I had worked for Bergdorf Goodman and I said, oh my, yes, and when he pressed me for details, I gave him a lot of phony dates.

He kept saying, "Really?" and, "That's very interesting," and finally he said, "Well, I know you're telling a great white lie because I was at Bergdorf's that whole time and I never laid eyes on you." Then he added with a twinkle, "But you've got the job."

After that we became great friends, and are to this day. I look Berny up every time I go to New York but he never lets me forget how I fibbed my way into *Roberta*. This was my second major break, for it led to a three-month contract which stretched into seven years.

*As this early
studio makeover shows,
it took a while to find
the "Lucille Ball" look,
circa 1935.*

C h a p t e r

5

♥

The next day I phoned home and told DeDe the bad news about losing my job. "Come anyway," I said, "but come by bus."

George Raft was then going with Virginia Peine, a friend of mine, and we often double-dated. When George heard that my family was arriving in Hollywood, that generous man insisted upon lending me his car and sixty-five dollars to welcome them in style. We could hardly greet the folks on bicycles. So in great glee, Freddy and I rolled off to the bus terminal in style.

When DeDe saw the little white bungalow on Ogden Drive in Hollywood, she burst into tears. This was one of the few times I ever saw her give way to her feelings. She came prepared to find work as a saleslady, armed with many written recommendations, but I put my foot down. Her working days were over, I told her.

In the warm sunshine, Daddy seemed to regain some of his old jaunty spirit. The milkman, the trash collector, the retired people on the block all became his fast friends, drinking coffee with him and listening to his political harangues in the garage. This was Daddy's workshop and also his office, complete with a desk and a couple of old chairs. I really think we added ten years to his life by moving him to California. And DeDe's migraine headaches eventually vanished.

Keeping that household afloat was the greatest thing that ever happened to me. I cherished every minute of it. It was tough going financially at times—I was earning only fifty dollars a week at RKO, and Freddy was making about the same—but it gave me a real purpose in life. I felt wanted and needed, and I was grateful to have the family together again.

Each morning I'd get up at six to reach the RKO studios on Gower Street by seven. The long, low plaster buildings of the old RKO lot house Desilu studios today. In fact, the same guard greets me at the front gate. When he says, "Hello, Lucy," these mornings, he reminds me that as an eager young starlet I disliked that nickname. My idols were Carole Lombard and Katharine Hepburn. I could visualize *Lucille* on theater marquees, but not *Lucy*.

So I wound up as a showgirl in *Roberta*, modeling clothes. The movie starred Fred Astaire and Ginger Rogers, the hottest song-and-dance team in Hollywood.

LOVE, LUCY

One of the clichés of Hollywood is "Behind every successful actress are a hairdresser and a mother." Hairdressers
come and go, but Ginger Rogers had only one fabulous
mother, a woman who played mother to many of us as we
worked our way up. Pandro Berman once remarked that Lela
Rogers charged about the set like a mother rhinoceros protecting her young. Lela was petite, dynamic, practical, and
shrewd. She was also quite as sexy and beautiful as her daughter. One way or another, Lela Rogers generally got her own
way.

Her daughter was her Galatea, a star she created. Ginger was just another bright-faced kid from Texas with one
Broadway show under her belt when she came to RKO. She
was not a great dancer and she couldn't sing or act. She had
to learn all these things and at the same time keep up with a
great performer, Fred Astaire, who was also one of the hardest taskmasters on earth. Fred would practice one dance step —
which would take about four seconds on the screen — for three
hours or more. He expected the same perfection from Ginger.
They'd dance sixteen, eighteen hours a day, until their feet
were literally bleeding.

Lela had started Ginger on the vaudeville circuit when
she was barely fourteen. Lela wrote her a new act every week,
including songs and dances, and made her costumes on a
portable sewing machine. She was her daughter's press agent,
business manager, and schoolteacher as well.

When I knew them, Lela was still keeping Ginger
hopping with lessons of all kinds: painting, sculpture, tennis;
geography, history, and the Great Books. Lela was great on

improving Ginger, or any of us who happened to be lucky enough to be around.

Ginger and Fred had little in common and battled through every picture, yet moviegoers found them one of the great romantic teams of all time. Hollywood at first didn't know what to make of Fred. He was skinny, balding, and treated girls like a kindly uncle. He had been in *Flying Down to Rio* with Dolores Del Rio. She wasn't a good dancer and was heavy at that time. Fred thought the finished movie was a bomb, so the studio decided to get him another girl and add some dance scenes. Fred asked for Ginger, having helped her in New York with some of her dance routines in *Girl Crazy* as a favor to George Gershwin. So a small part was added to *Flying Down to Rio* for Ginger, and overnight she and Fred were a hit. *The Gay Divorcee* followed.

Lela used to say that Ginger was Fred's best dancing partner because she imitated his body movements. When he danced with other girls, they took off and did their own kind of dancing. Ginger had no style of her own, so she borrowed Fred's. Then, to make him appear romantic, she never took her eyes off him. He gave her class as a dancer, and she gave him romantic appeal.

Just watching Lela handle Ginger on the set was an education in itself. Lela would go upstairs and say to the bosses, "You know, it would be a lot easier for Ginger if she had a little bit larger dressing room so she could wash her hair there instead of doing it at home. Ginger hasn't asked for this, but we could save forty-five minutes every morning if you'd just knock out a wall and give her a little more room."

Ginger was working so hard that she needed a few as-sists. She was a sunny, cheerful person, friendly and ap-proachable as a puppy. She never had an entourage to impress other people, as many stars did and still do. She needed a hair-dresser right at hand and a choreographer, and a secretary and a press man or two, and when she moved about the lot, they moved too, to save her time. When she walked from her dress-ing room to the set, seven or eight people came along. Ginger made seventy-one A movies in a period of fourteen years, in-cluding nine with Fred at RKO. When one of their films was finally in the can, Fred would sail to Europe to recuperate for six months; Ginger would start a new movie within twenty-four hours.

The wonderful thing about Lela was that she was "Mom" to a bevy of young struggling starlets. She directed RKO's Little Theater, where promising young people from other studios also came to be tutored by this wise, warm woman. When some young kid at Warner Bros. or MGM was hauled into the clink for drunken driving or some other charge, Mrs. Rogers was usually the first person the cops would tele-phone. "One of your kids is here," they'd tell her, "asking for Mom Rogers." And she'd drop everything and hurry to the po-lice station.

Just before we started filming *Roberta*, Lela got a phone call from Pan Berman at the front office. "We've put four models under a short-term contract for *Roberta*," he told her. "Three of them may be star material. Then there's a kid named Lucille Ball. Don't pay any attention to her. Berny Newman hired her, I don't know why. She's great at parties, a real funny kid, but I can't see any future for her in movies."

Lela thought otherwise. She told me years later, "I noticed the twinkle in your eyes, and the mobile face, which is a must for comedy. I also sensed a depth and a great capacity for love."

"What would you give to be a star in two years?" Lela asked me when I first was getting to know her.

I gulped and answered, "Gee, what d'ya mean?"

"Would you give me every breath you draw for two years? Will you work seven days a week? Will you sacrifice all your social life?"

I had observed Ginger's dedication on the set, and I knew that Lela meant every word. "I certainly will," I promised.

"Okay," she said, "let's start."

Lela was the first person to see me as a clown with glamour. She pulled my frizzy hair back off my brow and had a couple of my side teeth straightened. Then she sent me to a voice teacher, and told me to lower my high, squeaky voice by four tones.

Lela used to say, "A comedienne who does Ginger's style of comedy *has* to be good-looking. You should be able to sit and watch her read the telephone book, and with either Lucille or Ginger, you can."

Mrs. Rogers would arrive at her theater building on the RKO lot after lunch. Whoever wasn't working on some movie set would join her then; the rest would arrive at six p.m., when shooting generally stopped. To break down our reserve, she put us in improvisations. At three in the morning we'd be begging, "Oh, please, Mom . . . just one more . . . let's do just one more." Then we'd be going home at four, punchy with weariness but feeling so wonderful!

To me, the live theater is *it*, and still is. Lela mounted us in good plays and rehearsed us steadily for four or five months. Then we'd perform the play nightly except Sundays for the same length of time. Her productions were an incredible showcase for young talent. Admission to the plays was twenty-five cents. People flocked to our theater from all over town and from as far as New York. Often, we had directors and producers in the audience, and critics too. I met Brock Pemberton and his wife backstage one evening. For months after that, he tried to find me a part on Broadway.

I soon became part of a small, intimate group centered around Ginger, who was about my age. On weekends we played tennis, went swimming, and double-dated at the Ambassador and the Biltmore. The group included Phyllis Fraser, Ginger's first cousin, who is now Mrs. Bennett Cerf; Eddie Rubin; Florence Lake; and Anita "the Face" Colby. Ginger was dating Lee Bowman, Henry Fonda, Jimmy Stewart, and Orson Welles; often I went along.

It was such a busy, happy time for me. Lela took the dungarees off us and put us into becoming dresses; she ripped off our hair bands and made us do our hair right. If we went to see a big producer in his office, she cautioned us to put on full makeup and look like somebody. She made us read good literature to improve our English and expand our understanding of character.

She drummed into us how to treat agents and the

bosses upstairs. Lela believed that sex is more of a hindrance than a help to a would-be star. More actresses have made it to the top *without* obvious sex appeal than *with* it. Lela taught us to dedicate ourselves to our work and to ignore the nerve-racking rumors of calamity issuing from the front office. I never played politics at RKO, and it wouldn't have helped if I had. RKO had eleven presidents in fourteen years. Lela advised us to work on ourselves and pay no attention to those corporate machinations.

Lela wouldn't tolerate anyone taking advantage of her charges. One producer at RKO kept sending her his protégées to include in her classes. Lela kept throwing them out, until her patience was exhausted. One day another protégée arrived, saying coyly, "Mr. X sent me."

Lela picked up a telephone and told that producer, "I am not Madam Rogers, and my workshop is not a whorehouse. This girl you sent me today has no talent whatsoever and no future in the theater. So put her where you had her last night and keep her there." That was the last we saw of those gamy dames.

My first contract at RKO was for three months; this was extended to six months, and then to a year. On May 12, 1935, our "Cleo-baby" turned sixteen and was finally allowed to choose where she wanted to live. She immediately left her father in Buffalo and joined us in Hollywood. Cleo was so happy to have a mother again she wouldn't let DeDe out of her sight.

I drove directly from the studio to the bus terminal to

get her in my secondhand Studebaker Phaeton, my first car. Cleo was overwhelmed at the sight of a "real movie star" in full stage makeup, false lashes, big picture hat, and polka-dot silk dress. I was back to making seventy-five dollars a week and thought I had arrived.

My contract had been extended to a year, but as 1935 drew to an end, Lela found me in tears. "Last night at midnight was the last hour they could pick up my option," I told her. "I guess I'm through."

Lela stormed up to the front office and learned that indeed I had been dropped. A new president had been installed and was effecting "economies" by cutting down the payroll.

"Very well." Lela shrugged. "If Lucille goes, I go. She's the best student I've got. I'll take her to some other studio and manage her like I do Ginger."

The bosses paled at this threat, and I was immediately rehired. Lela told me that the legal department had made a mistake about the date of the option. "They may ask you to take the same salary, without a raise this year," she added. "And if I were you, I'd take it."

So there I was, safe for another year. Lela taught us never to see anyone as bigger or more important than ourselves, but she discouraged outbursts of petty temperament. It was very bad, she said, for a young player to get the reputation of being "difficult." This was brought home to me one time when my hot temper got out of hand.

I was sitting before a makeup table one morning when the head makeup man, Mel Burns, rudely told me to get out;

Katharine Hepburn was on her way down. She had been hired at $2,000 a week and was held in great awe and respect by everyone on the lot. So with one eyebrow and no lipstick on my face, I hurriedly gathered up my things and left. After Mel Burns started working on Hepburn, however, I realized I had left my eyebrow pencil behind.

I came back drinking a cup of coffee and stuck my head through the little talking hole into the dressing room. Mel Burns ignored my polite request for the eyebrow pencil and went on applying makeup to Hepburn. I asked him again, and then a third time. He made some stale reply. I had been putting up with this guy for a long time and had had about enough. Suddenly the coffee cup left my hand and went sailing into the dressing room, narrowly missing Hepburn's celebrated head.

A little later, Lela was summoned to the front office. "This Lucille Ball is temperamental—we'll have to get rid of her," Mr. Berman said.

"Of course she's temperamental, or she wouldn't be worth a cent to you or anybody else," Lela flared up. "So is Mel Burns, so if you fire her, fire them both."

I was in the doghouse all right, so to show everybody whose side she was on, Lela took me to the commissary for lunch. Hepburn walked over to our table and said soothingly, "It's all right, Lucy." Then she added, "You have to wait until you get a little bigger before you can practice temperament."

Lela expected all of us to show up at play rehearsals, whether we were in the production or not. As Phil Silvers is fond of saying, "If you hang around show business long enough, you learn!" We all spent hours and hours in the darkened theater watching rehearsals.

We were putting on *A Case of Rain,* with Anita Colby in the lead, when Lela called me at ten o'clock one morning. "Anita's sick and can't go on tonight," she announced. "Will you take her place?"

She then explained that there was no time for a full rehearsal. "My assistant will go through the lines and moves with you," she said.

I had, of course, studied the play, and watched the rehearsals, but there's a big difference between this kind of mental approach and the actual performance. I arrived at Lela's theater about eleven a.m. and stayed there all day, until the opening at eight o'clock that night. I don't know how I did it, but I played the lead without missing a line or a cue, and got twenty-five more laughs than usual.

Afterward Lela came to me and said, "Lucille, if you're in the theater for fifty years, you'll never face a more difficult task. You've been through the worst that can happen to a performer. I hope you'll always rise to challenges like that."

Only recently did I learn from Lela that my jumping in at the last moment was her way of testing me. Anita's sudden "illness" was a put-up job.

Sitting in the back row of Lela's Little Theater one night was Pandro Berman. He was short, dark, vital, and still in his early thirties, the boy wonder of the industry. He produced all the Astaire-Rogers musicals and had often been locked in mortal combat with Lela over Ginger's lines or dances or her attention-getting costumes. One of Ginger's bouffant ostrich-feather dance gowns almost suffocated skinny Fred. But Lela fought Pan Berman for every feather, and won.

As RKO's top producer started to leave the theater after the performance, Lela came up to him and crowed, "That was Lucille Ball who played the lead tonight on only a few hours' notice. She's the girl you said had no acting potential."

For once, Mr. Berman had no counterattack to the "mother rhinoceros." "Yes, I know," he told Lela quietly, and stole away.

Lela kept telling the RKO producers and directors, "I have a passel of good talent, and when you're casting bit parts, I want you to use my students." Director Mark Sandrich came to her one day when he was casting *Top Hat,* and Lela talked him into giving me a few lines. It was my first real speaking part, and during the filming I was so nervous and unstrung that I couldn't get the words out. They phoned Lela and told her I wasn't doing well and would have to be replaced. So Lela hied herself right over to the set.

My scene took place in a florist's shop, where I was supposed to make some biting remarks to some man about Fred's sending flowers to Ginger. I stumbled and blew my lines until Lela said to Mark Sandrich, "Reverse the lines. It's not in character for the girl to make those biting remarks. . . . Give them to the man." So we reversed the dialogue and everything worked out fine.

My next movie was *Follow the Fleet,* which was another big splashy Astaire-Rogers musical, with Betty Grable in one of her early parts. Ginger and Fred sang and danced to Irving Berlin's "Let's Face the Music and Dance," "I'm Putting All My Eggs in One Basket," "We Saw the Sea," and "Let Yourself Go." It was based on the stage comedy *Shore Leave*, with little plot but great songs and dancing. I played Ginger's friend. The picture opened at Radio City Music Hall in February 1936, and shortly afterward I got my first fan letter, which I still have. It was addressed to the front office, and said, "You might give the tall, gum-chewing blonde more parts and see if she can't make the grade—a good gamble."

From *Follow the Fleet*, I went into the second lead of *That Girl from Paris*, with Lily Pons and Jack Oakie. On the set, I clowned continually. One day an older man came up to me and said, "Young lady, if you play your cards right, you can be one of the greatest comediennes in the business." I just gave him a look. I figured he was one of those guys who came around measuring starlets for tights. Then I learned he was Edward Sedgwick, a famous comedy director who had coached Buster Keaton and Jack Haley. Eventually, Ed Sedgwick taught me many comedy techniques—the double take and the eye-rolling bit and how to handle props. He became Desi's mentor, and his wonderful, witty wife, Ebba, my confidante. They were both as close as father and mother to us.

Russell Markert, Lela Rogers, Ed Sedgwick—these were but a few of the experienced theater people who generously gave me a boost. I have a theory about the assists we get in life. Only rarely can we repay those people who helped us, but we can pass that help along to others. That's why, in 1958,

I reactivated Lela's theater workshop with two dozen talented kids trying to get started in show business. My accountants referred to it as "Lucy's Folly," but Marie Torre called it "the most practical workshop in television." I found it a deeply satisfying experience. It was my way of thanking Lela.

Freddy, Cleo, DeDe, Daddy, and I were all still living in the little three-bedroom rented house at 1344 North Ogden Drive with two fox terriers and five white cats. In the same way that I collected animals, Daddy built up a large circle of ne'er-do-wells and underdogs.

He suffered a slight stroke at seventy-one, and afterward became garrulous and even more worried about the state of the world. My dates thought him eccentric and a "character," especially when he read aloud to them from the *Daily Worker* while they waited for me.

There's no doubt that Daddy's experience with the law in Celoron disillusioned him deeply about democracy. He had worked hard all his life; then overnight everything was taken away from him, unjustly. During the Depression he saw many of his closest friends also lose their homes and life savings through circumstances beyond their control. The furniture factories in Jamestown closed, the craftsmen were thrown out of work, and after a few weeks or months, most of them were penniless and on relief. And these were master craftsmen: proud, able men.

Daddy would complain about the hard lot of the workingman, and before we knew it, his garage became the meeting place of radical left-wingers and crackpots. I never saw any of these people, being much too busy working, but DeDe often said that they were taking advantage of Daddy's warm heart. He was the softest touch in the whole neighborhood.

He would go to the relief board and battle for a total stranger. He was a sincere humanitarian, but also sentimental and unrealistic. For instance, he soon discovered that the corner of Fairfax and Sunset Boulevard, just a block from our house, was a favorite gathering spot of Hollywood's call girls. Daddy would hurry over to some lady of the evening and press a five-dollar bill into her hand, saying, "Take this and go back home. You don't have to work tonight."

"Sure, pop, thanks a lot," the woman would say. She'd pocket the money, walk around the block, and be back at the same stand five minutes later. Daddy gave away his money every week, until we finally had to stop giving him any.

If we contradicted or crossed him, he became highly emotional. It was easier to agree with him than to risk his having a second stroke. We couldn't keep a maid because he'd immediately tell her she was overworked and underpaid. I got him a job in the carpentry department at RKO where master woodcraftsmen were scarce. He worked one Monday, from seven until eleven a.m. It took him exactly that long to walk the wood turners out on strike—and they were getting very good money. Until Daddy arrived, it had never entered their minds they were the least bit underpaid.

After his stroke, Daddy was confined a good deal to a rocking chair. There was a tall tree near our sidewalk which he said interfered with his view of the mountains. "That goddamn tree is in my way," he complained repeatedly. "I'm going to cut it down." I explained this would be against the law. "It's not our tree," I told him. "It belongs to the city."

A few weeks later, he changed his tune. "Someday that tree will blow down in a storm, you'll see." Sure enough, during a mild sprinkle, the tree toppled over. Then we could see that the roots had been cut, the sod neatly turned back for the operation and then replaced. Worse than that, the tree fell right on top of my new secondhand Studebaker, which was parked at the curb. It cost me four hundred dollars to get it fixed.

I was going at such a pace at the studio and in Lela's Little Theater around this time that I wore myself down to 100 pounds. My normal weight today is 130. While I was in the hospital on a fattening diet, Lela asked me if I wanted a bit part in a play by Bartlett Cormack, *Hey Diddle Diddle*, which was headed for Broadway. Lela developed not only actors and actresses, but playwrights too. It never hurts a movie actress to appear in a successful play back east, so I jumped at the chance.

It was not a great play, but I enjoyed the junket. Conway Tearle was the star, and Alice White played a starlet in this feeble melodrama about life on Eucalyptus Drive in Hollywood. Keenan Wynn, a massive talent with a daredevil personality, was a "man in white."

We opened the show in Princeton, and the reviewers called me "another Hepburn." We moved on to New Haven, and there Conway Tearle became seriously ill, so that was the end of the tour.

L O V E , L U C Y

In New York I moved into a swank Fifty-seventh Street hotel, and then walked over to Fifth Avenue to buy myself a truckload of new clothes. To a newspaper reporter for a New York paper, I said candidly, "I'm happy for the first time in my life. I know what I'm doing and where I'm going." I explained that I had been in love twice but that I didn't want to get married. "I want to be a good comedienne," I told that reporter, "like Alice Brady or ZaSu Pitts. Character actresses last longer."

After my big clothes spree, I went up to Jamestown to visit my grandmother Peterson. It was February and six inches of fresh snow lay on the ground, to my intense delight. I saw Johnny briefly. He had not married and was still carrying the torch for me, but my feeling for him had cooled to a very small glow of affection. With the arrival of the Depression, Johnny had fallen on hard times. Jamestown was a sad place that winter of 1937. The furniture business was in the complete doldrums; the banks had foreclosed on four thousand homes and thrown as many families into the street. Johnny asked me for money to pay for his mother's insurance, and I was glad to be able to help him. It was wonderful to be a contract player; whether you worked or not, you got that paycheck every week.

Back in Hollywood, I did another play for Lela, *Breakfast for Venora.* After the last performance, as I was removing my stage makeup, Lela came backstage with a huge bouquet of red roses. "These are for you," she said.

"But Lela," I said, amazed, "what for?"

"Tonight's our last night together," explained Lela.

"I've taught you everything I can. From now on, you have to put it into practice."

I could feel the tears welling up inside me. "You mean I'm not coming back anymore?" I asked incredulously.

"No, darling," said Lela. "I've had you two years, and the studio says that's all. They've got some new students for me. You're through here at the Little Theater."

We both cried a little and then I didn't see Lela for weeks. As a final favor, she got me a speaking part in *Stage Door*, which Gregory La Cava directed. He was an outstanding director, but he didn't particularly like me; he'd only given me the part, I'm sure, at Lela's prodding.

The movie was based on the play by Edna Ferber and George Kaufman about a group of stagestruck girls living together at the Footlights Club. Critic Howard Barnes called it "brilliantly written, directed and acted . . . a superbly modulated succession of scenes and moods." He added that "Ginger Rogers as Katharine Hepburn's caustic roommate serves notice that she can act as well as dance." Adolphe Menjou played the rake play producer and Gail Patrick the opportunistic young girl. Andrea Leeds was the overly sensitive one who committed suicide. Eve Arden and Ann Miller and so many other fine actors had roles in this picture. It was a treat to be even a *part* of it.

I played one of the boarders at the Footlights Club, wearing my hair long and dark, loose and straight like Hepburn's. It was my first standout part, and afterward some Hollywood producer's wife lunching at Chasen's was overheard to say, "Who was that funny, tall girl in *Stage Door* who went home to Oregon to marry a lumberman?"

My next opus was also a big, expensive A movie, *Having Wonderful Time.* Ginger Rogers and Douglas Fairbanks, Jr., played the leads in this comedy about two weeks at Camp Kare Free. Eve Arden, who had been in *Stage Door* with me, was in the large cast, as well as Phyllis Fraser, Jack Carson, and a new comic named Red Skelton. I even got Cleo a small part. We went on location for three weeks to seven-thousand-foot Big Bear Mountain. I felt literally on top of the world. The movie was a hit at Radio City, and for the first time I was mentioned in the New York movie reviews: "Lucille Ball is faultless as Miriam, one of the harpies."

*R*adio gave Lucille
*the audience recognition
and acclaim that had
so far eluded her in movies.*

Chapter 6

♥

I believe that we're as happy in life as we make up our minds to be. All actors and actresses, no matter how talented or famous, have ups and downs in their careers. It's just the nature of the business. You have to learn to roll with the punches, and not take them personally. Ed Sedgwick and Buster Keaton used to tell me about dozens of Hollywood people who ran into trouble. This was comforting, like reading an autobiography and thinking, "Well, that happened to them, too. . . . I'm not the only one."

At RKO I was known as the starlet who never complained. When I began getting small supporting parts in big A movies like *Stage Door* and *Having Wonderful Time,* the front-office brass began to notice me. There was an important producer who was especially kind and encouraging. I liked him and respected his judgment. He had a young wife and small children, and we often spoke about the problems of raising a family.

Then—I don't know quite how it happened—this producer fell in love with me. He wanted to divorce his wife, leave his children, go against his religion and his conscience to marry me.

To me, marriage has always meant sharing. It meant forever, like the wonderful marriage of my grandparents Flora Belle and Fred. Theirs wasn't a storybook romance, by any means; they had plenty of yelling fights—"You come right in here, Fred," and, "I'll be damned if I will," and so forth—but I knew as a child that no force on heaven or earth would be strong enough to pull those two apart.

That's the kind of marriage I wanted. I respected this producer's talent; he was attractive, young, and vital. But I couldn't allow myself to fall in love with him because of his wife and children.

But because I was ambitious, and because he was a great catch, I struggled with my conscience long and painfully. Friends told me, "Why don't you marry him? He's a real talent, and he'll make your career." But in the end, I finally found the courage to turn him down.

This decision put into motion a lot of unforeseen consequences. The producer, of course, suffered from a bad case of wounded pride; he immediately lost all interest in me and my career. But his wife heard some studio gossip—after the romance was busted and over—and really lowered the boom. She had influence through some important relatives, so that she was able to decree that one Lucille Ball would never again appear in any A picture at RKO.

Then all my friends said, "You dope! If you'd married the guy, you'd be on top. Now you'll never make it at RKO, and the wife will get all the other Hollywood wives to black-ball you so that no other major studio will hire you."

My movie career just about ended then and there, but I never regretted that decision. I knew what it was like to lose a beloved father early in life; no child was going to be put through that torture because of me.

When a man and woman work in close proximity in the highly charged atmosphere of moviemaking, emotions become very combustible. I remember Humphrey Bogart at a garden party, watching the beautiful actresses in their diaphanous gowns walk by with their handsome actor escorts, and saying to me with a wink, "No wonder they all want to f＿ ＿ each other all the time."

But actors and actresses learn to switch their emotions on and off like light bulbs. Change, not constancy, characterizes the usual Hollywood romance. This producer's temporary interest in me caused a big roadblock in my career for a while. But I was convinced that eventually I would get going again. In the meantime, I had to give Hollywood a rest and look around for other showcases for my talent. I wound up trying radio. This turned out to be one of the smartest things I ever did.

Early in 1938, I appeared on Jack Haley's weekly radio program, *The Wonder Show.* This led to a featured spot on Phil Baker's Hollywood radio show. I worked with some wonderful comics, Jack Carson and Al Pierce, as well as Jack Haley and Phil Baker. This gave me a name in the trade as a good feminine foil. I could flip a comedy line, which a lot of actresses couldn't do. In radio I couldn't depend upon props or costumes or makeup; I had to rely on timing and tone of voice for comic effects, and this was invaluable training.

My contract at RKO still had some time to run, and since I was well liked on the lot, I soon became known as "Queen of the B's." My first B picture, made on a low budget with little-known stars but with a strong story line, was *Next Time I Marry.* James Ellison and Lee Bowman starred in it with me, and our director was Garson Kanin. One reviewer wrote, "Miss Ball, the former lanky and glass-eyed comedienne, has prettied herself up, put her eyebrows in the wrong place, and acquits herself with charm and gusto." My radio work had put new zip in my acting, and besides, Garson Kanin was a good director. *New York Times* critic Bosley Crowther called *Next Time I Marry* "one of the best 'B' comedies of the year."

Next I was cast in the Annabel series with Jack Oakie. The first was *The Affairs of Annabel,* in which I was a glamorous movie star and a comic foil for Jack. When this did well at the box office, we made *Annabel Takes a Tour.* My old beau Ralph Forbes was in this second picture, playing a rakish viscount.

I also did some musicals with Kay Kyser. My option was picked up each year with an automatic increase in salary, so that eventually my little $50 a week rose to $1,000.

I began dating a director, who was twenty years my senior. Al Hall was part of the Charlie Ruggles, Buster Keaton, Ed Sedgwick, and Bill and Mary Gargan group. They were all wonderful to me. We did things together, almost like a family. Al had been married to Lola Lane, and was in no hurry to marry again; I enjoyed his company, his advice and guidance, but was not in love with him. For two years or so we had a perfect understanding, with no demands on either side. This easy, relaxed relationship continued until a Cuban skyrocket burst over my horizon.

In 1939 I felt sufficiently affluent to buy my first fur coat, a great bushy silver fox with square shoulders four feet wide. I also hired my first personal maid, Harriet McCain. I first heard Harriet being interviewed on a radio program called *Help Thy Neighbor.* She said that her mother had worked for the Jack Bennys for fourteen years and that she was looking for the same kind of job. When I interviewed Harriet, I didn't ask for any references, to her surprise. After about five minutes' talk, I decided I liked her looks and manner and asked, "What size uniform do you wear?" and that was that. She has been with me throughout the United States and Europe—traveling in the air, on the sea, and on the ground—and at home and on movie sets and backstage at the theater for twenty-three years.

When I was doing *Wildcat* on Broadway in 1960 and 1961 and living in an Upper East Side apartment house, I was told that Negroes were not allowed to ride the front elevator. But I changed that rule in a hurry. Harriet and I were the first to integrate those $1,300-a-month apartments, I'm glad to say.

Back in 1939, Harriet would arrive at my house early in the morning to fix coffee and help me get dressed. Then we'd drive to the RKO studios in my bright red Buick convertible. There, Harriet would cook me a hearty breakfast: steak, fried potatoes, hot biscuits—the works. Lupe Velez, who had to starve herself continually to keep her curves under control, would sweep into my dressing room stamping and swearing, "Goddammit, Lucille, you and your breakfasts!"

Carole Lombard also dropped in often. She was so elegant; her clothes looked as if they had been poured on her. I tried to copy the way she looked, but not the way she talked. Carole had a very lively vocabulary. She could get away with it. Not everybody can and I didn't even try. But there were many things about Carole that were, oh-boy-out-of-this-world wonderful. She was class. She was a good actress, and she always looked great. More important, she had a lot of heart. No wonder Clark Gable adored her so.

When I'm weighing a particularly difficult decision, sometimes I ask myself what Carole would have said, and it helps. She gave me lots of pointers on what she called "studio behavior."

Often, Harriet and I had a two-hour drive up into the mountains or sagebrush country or wherever they were shooting outdoor scenes. We had to be at the studio by four forty-five a.m. in order to be ready to leave for location by seven.

The Hunt family, "Grandpa" Fred C. Hunt (far left) and "Grandma" Flora Belle Orcutt Hunt (far right, seated), who were Lucille's surrogate parents while her mother, "DeDe" (far right, standing), was away working. Others in the picture are Lola and Harold Hunt (DeDe's siblings) and Eveline Bailey Hunt (Lucille's great-grandmother).

Henry Durrell Ball, Lucille's father, circa 1910.

Lucille at age four with Aunt Lola in Jamestown, 1915.

At two, Lucille sports a serious hair ribbon and an attitude to match, 1913.

Grandpa Fred C. Hunt, whom Lucille called "Daddy," circa 1935.

Lucille coupled her beauty and her intelligence and set out "to make some noise," which echoes still around the world.

Lucille, home from New York, recovering from an unusual form of arthritis.

Lucille and her pal Marion Strong, on their first venture into New York City.

Lucille (left page) quickly moved uptown to Hattie Carnegie's salon, circa 1932.

Under the careful grooming of the studio, Lucille quickly found her place in the Hollywood sun.

Lucille's younger brother, Fred, had a number of jobs in Hollywood, including the management of Desi's road tours, and later Desi's Palm Springs hotel.

Lucille with James Ellison, in You Can't Fool Your Wife, *1940.*

On the town with her beau of five years, director Alexander Hall, circa 1939 (left page).

As a burlesque dancer, Lucille spins in the spotlight of Dance, Girl, Dance, *1940. Her facial expression hints that she was also in a spin of another kind — having just met Desi Arnaz!*

PTEMBER 15. 1940

LUCILLE BALL
of the movies, dances in the spot.
that's no waltz she's doing.

Studio publicity shots like this were more exciting to the public because of Lucille and Desi's real-life romance.

Lucille and Desi met on the set of Too Many Girls, *the picture that brought them together in 1940.*

One of hundreds of telegrams sent coast-to-coast during their brief, but intense, courtship.

BY DIRECT WIRE FROM
WESTERN UNION

SC1 12 TOUR=CP NEWYORK NY OCT 1 1940 1054A
LUCILLE BALL=RKO STUDIOS=

BABY ILL SEE YOU TOMORROW WILL WIRE DEFINITE TIME OF
ARRIVAL LOVE=
    DESI.

At the El Morocco in New York, Lucille and Desi sadly ponder the reasons they must never marry — one week before they elope!

*Shortly after their marriage,
Lucille and Desi make time for
a photo session at the Pierre Hotel, 1940.
(Photo by Jimmy Sileo.)*

Lucille and Desi disembark from the Super Chief in Hollywood at the end of their honeymoon.

Mr. and Mrs. Arnaz in an unguarded moment at their favorite Palm Springs bungalow.

*Lucille and her beloved dogs atop the barbecue
that Desi designed and built at Chatsworth,
to remind him of Cuba.*

Although giving Desi a hand painting the trellis, Lucille's interests were decorating the house and gardening, while Desi had talent as a builder, 1942.

The pool at Chatsworth, a favorite meeting place for Lucille, Desi, and their friends, circa 1942.

A scene from one of the frequent costume parties given by Lucille and Desi at the Desilu Ranch, 1942. Lucille, second from left, stands behind legendary actor Lionel Barrymore.

Always on the guest list for their many parties were dear friends comedy film director Ed Sedgwick and his wife, Ebba.

Lucille with Grandpa Hunt and DeDe, followed by Desi and other family members, who were always welcome at Chatsworth.

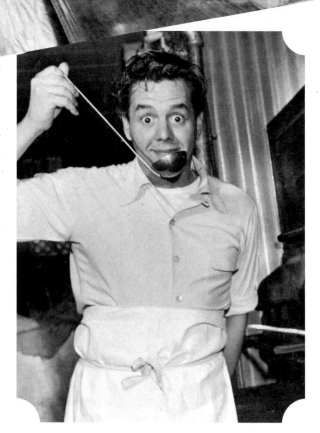

Magazine photographers were always posing Lucille and Desi in typical domestic situations. Here, they reverse the expected, since in the Arnaz household Desi was the real cook.

Desi's spaghetti sauce was legendary, and he would never serve it until it was just right.

Sometimes a day that began at four a.m. ended at two a.m. the following day if we stayed on location for night scenes. To alleviate the tedium of endlessly waiting between scenes, Harriet and I played gin and poker.

To Harriet's way of thinking, I didn't act like a potential movie star at all. I'd get ferociously hungry out there in the sagebrush, and since I had trouble keeping my weight up, I'd send Harriet to the food wagon for fried-potato sandwiches. Harriet was ashamed to give such an order; she felt I should be nibbling on lettuce leaves and cottage cheese like the other players. But she soon learned that I like only the plain and hearty foods.

But those long hours of waiting and of takes and retakes made me restless. My nerves would get frayed and I'd become irritated and short-tempered. After one of my outbursts, Harriet would go around apologizing for me. "Miss Ball didn't mean it. . . . She's not really mad at you, she's just hungry."

I was almost twenty-eight and hungry for a lot of things: the deep, enduring love of a man I could love in return, and children, and recognition as a performer. I was earning a very high salary: $1,000 a week for forty weeks of the year at the studio, whether I worked or not, plus my radio earnings. But I knew something was missing from my life.

In the spring of 1939, I was offered a small dramatic part in a B movie, *Five Came Back*. My role was originally intended for Ann Sothern, but she was too busy to do it, so somebody thought of me. I had done only comedy, but luckily I had a great director, John Farrow, and he helped me realize one of the best parts of my movie career.

Five Came Back was a sleeper which proved to be a
solid-gold hit. When it opened, the Rialto in New York went
on a twenty-four-hour schedule to accommodate the crowds.
It was the film that gave my career a much-needed boost. Soon
I was being told that the front office was "grooming" me for A
films and stardom at last. In line with this, I was sent east in
December for personal appearances. "And while you're in New
York," the studio head told me, "be sure and see the big Broadway hit *Too Many Girls.* We've bought the movie rights, and
George Abbott will direct. You may get a starring role in it."

In New York, the studio press agents wanted to photograph me on the outdoor rink at Rockefeller Plaza doing a
pratfall on the ice. I said sure, why not, and bought myself a
short black velvet skating outfit trimmed with white fur, and
a pair of long black tights. Russell Markert told me for God's
sake not to go through with the stunt. He knew I'd do almost
anything for a laugh, but he also knew I was no acrobat.

"You don't know how to fall properly," he warned
me. "You're apt to hurt yourself."

I should have listened to him, but in those days I
thought I was indestructible. After so many years in California
I guess I'd forgotten how hard ice can be. I fell over backward
and landed with a mighty crack on my sacroiliac. I made all the
big dailies in New York, all right, and the rest of the country,
too. They had to carry me off the rink on a stretcher, and I spent
the next ten days of my New York holiday in a hospital.

From show business friends who popped in and out of my hospital room, I learned that the new Broadway musical *Too Many Girls* was a great hit. It was fast-paced and funny, with gorgeous girls and Rodgers and Hart songs. The sensation of the show, everyone agreed, was a twenty-two-year-old Cuban named Desi Arnaz.

The plot of *Too Many Girls* wasn't much: A beautiful rich girl decides to go to college, and she takes along four football heroes who are really her bodyguards in disguise. Desi was cast as the South American football wonder; he sang with a heavy Spanish accent, danced a way-out conga, banged a bongo drum, and strummed a guitar. From the way girls reacted to him, he was the Elvis Presley of his day. Offstage he was dating film stars, stage stars, and all the leading debutantes, including the beautiful Brenda Frazier.

My friends told me that this young nightclub entertainer was a nice guy and that his overnight success on Broadway hadn't gone to his head at all. In his review of *Too Many Girls*, critic John Mason Brown called Desi "at once attractive and modest," and in *Variety,* John Anderson wrote that in the title song, "the 'Sta-combed' Desi Arnaz establishes his position as the show's glamour boy and clinches the Latin-It supremacy on Broadway without reducing the part to a gigolodeon."

When I recovered enough to hobble around, Russell Markert took me to see *Too Many Girls*. I couldn't take my eyes off this Desi Arnaz. A striped football jersey hugged his big shoulders and chest, while those narrow hips in tight football pants swayed to the catchy rhythms of the bongo drum he was carrying. I recognized the kind of electrifying charm that can never be faked: star quality.

Then Desi opened his mouth and began talking in his own peculiar brand of broken English, and a great belly laugh burst out of me. Now it's hard to make me laugh. I observe, I smile, but when I'm really amused you can hear me a block away. Here was a stunning-looking male who was not only thrilling but funny. What a combination!

Russell asked me where I wanted to go after the show, and I said La Conga. That's where Desi was appearing nightly after the show, singing and demonstrating the conga, then the sexiest and hottest dance in the country. But that particular night was Desi's night off, so I didn't get to meet him.

In a few days, I went back to Hollywood. *Too Many Girls* was doing such a sell-out business in New York that it would be months before George Abbott would be free to do the movie, so in the meantime, the studio gave me a co-starring role with Maureen O'Hara in *Dance, Girl, Dance.*

Now, I discovered long ago that when you're cast in a part, first you're cast physically. The producer couldn't care less about your soul shining from your big bright eyes; he looks to see if you're thin or fat, young or old, ugly or beautiful. I'm tall and wear clothes well, so first I was cast as a showgirl and a clotheshorse. Then I played the other woman, the prostitute, and the hard-as-nails career girl. I guess I'm not the lady type. The refined-looking Maureen O'Hara got the role of the ballet dancer in *Dance, Girl, Dance;* I was the tough, wisecracking stripteaser.

L O V E ,   L U C Y

One reviewer said of *Dance, Girl, Dance,* "Miss O'Hara, after the usual mishaps, realizes her ambition to become a ballet dancer and Lucille Ball, her rival, becomes the sort of woman other women describe in a single word. Nevertheless, it is Miss Ball who brings an occasional zest into the film, especially that appearance in the burlesque temple where she stripteases."

We were filming this scene the day I first met Desi, on the RKO lot. I was wearing a slinky gold lamé dress slit up to my thigh, and my long reddish-gold hair fell over my bare shoulders. I also sported a fake black eye, where my lover had supposedly socked me.

George Abbott, who was lunching at the studio commissary with the New York cast of *Too Many Girls,* called me over. Desi reared back at the sight of me. "Whatta honk of a woman!" he gasped.

At the end of the day's shooting, I was in slacks and a sweater, my face washed and my long red hair pulled neatly back in a bow. Desi didn't recognize me as the wild woman he had met at lunch, and had to be introduced all over again. He invited me to dinner and I accepted.

We went to a nightclub, but instead of joining the conga line we sat at a small table, talking and talking. I might as well admit here and now I fell in love with Desi wham, bang! In five minutes. There was only one thing better than looking at Desi, and that was talking to him.

Desi's real name, he told me, rolling all his *r*'s magnificently, was Desiderio Alberto Arnaz y de Acha III. He was an only child and born with the proverbial silver spoon in his mouth. His family owned cattle ranches and townhouses in Cuba. Desi's father, a doctor of pharmacology, was mayor of Santiago for ten years; his mother, Delores, was a famous beauty and one of the heirs to the Bacardi rum fortune.

At sixteen, Desi had his own speedboat and motorcar and three different homes. He had never faced a worry or a strain. He loved his life, and everyone loved him.

Then came one of those revolutions that frequently erupted in Cuba. Desi and his mother were alone at one of the family ranches when he awoke to shouts and gunfire. From the window he could see soldiers on horseback slaughtering cattle and setting fire to outbuildings. Desi's father was in Havana at the time, six hundred miles away at the other end of the island.

Desi's mother ran through the house collecting all the loose cash she could find and her pet Chihuahua. A cousin arrived just in time to rush them into safe hiding. Desi and his mother, looking back, saw their house in flames.

"*Mi casa!*" she screamed and screamed until it was out of sight.

Whenever they passed rebel soldiers, to avoid attack (or recognition) Desi would wave and shout, "*Viva la revolución!*" He and his mother stayed in hiding in an aunt's house in Havana for six months. Desi's father, along with the rest of the Cuban Senate, was locked up in the Morro Castle fortress.

All the family property was confiscated; they lost everything. When he was finally released, Desi's father decided to go to Florida and start over. Desi would join him soon.

Mrs. Arnaz would stay with a sister in Cuba until they had enough money saved to send for her.

Desi was seventeen when he arrived penniless in Miami, with only the clothes on his back. He found his father in a dingy rooming house, heating canned beans on a hot plate. But even this place was more than they could afford, so they moved into an unheated warehouse filled with rats. When Desi saw his father—the former mayor of Santiago, one of Cuba's biggest cities—chasing rats with a stick, he put his head in his hands and cried.

As he told me the story, Desi's eyes filled with tears. I began to sniffle too, thinking about my own grandfather and how his life had been ruined through no fault of his own. I knew just how Desi felt.

Though just a kid, and with only a few words of English, Desi hadn't sat around feeling sorry for himself and waiting for the welfare workers. He went out to look for a job—any job. He earned his first money cleaning out canary cages for a pet store. Next he drove a banana truck.

Desi had been attending the Colegio de Dolores in Santiago, and eventually graduated from St. Patrick's High School in Miami with A's in English and American history. He was nominated "most courteous" of his class. Desi's parents had taught him good manners; driving trucks and taxis after school didn't change his gentlemanly ways.

In 1936, when Desi was nineteen, he heard that a big-time rumba band at the famous Roney-Plaza in Miami Beach needed a singing guitarist. In a dress suit borrowed for the one-night tryout, Desi got shakily to his feet and sang what was later to become his signature song, the weird and wonderful "Babalu." He couldn't have known he'd wind up crooning that song about ten thousand more times. Desi and "Babalu" are sort of like Judy Garland and "Over the Rainbow."

The applause almost knocked Desi over. Then he looked up and saw dozens of his former classmates from St. Patrick's High in the audience with their parents. Desi, being Desi, started to cry; the audience clapped harder than ever, and Desi was hired. The pay was no great shakes—fifty dollars a week—but the first thing Desi did was send for his mother. But his father had fallen in love with an American woman who wasn't about to be relegated to a Latin man's *casa chica,* so his parents were divorced shortly thereafter and he gallantly assumed the responsibility of supporting his mother from that day forward.

One night while Desi was at the Plaza, Xavier Cugat caught his act and asked him to audition. Cugat gave him a job as a singer traveling around the country, but he wasn't paid nearly as much as he knew he was worth. Eventually Desi decided to quit and go back to Miami with his mother and start a band of his own.

He soon learned that in striking out on your own, you have to throw out your chest and sell yourself. The Depression was still hanging on and band jobs were scarce.

One day, Desi found himself down to his last ten dollars. Desi's a gambler at heart, so with his pockets full of his Cugat press clippings, he strutted into Mother Kelley's and ordered filet mignon, champagne, cherries Jubilee, and a big two-dollar Havana cigar. When the manager stopped by his table, Desi pulled out his clippings. Cugat was begging him to return, he bragged, but he wanted to start his own band. Before the evening was over, the manager had hired Desi to organize a Latin band for a new nightclub he was opening.

Cugat sent him some musicians—none of whom played Latin music. They were billed as the Siboney Septet, although there were actually only five members. Desi sang and played the guitar. "We sounded so terrible," he told me on our first date, "that to entertain the publeek, I start them doing *la conga*. Thees ees a dance we do in Santiago de Cuba at carnival time. You get in a beeg line and hold the heeps of the girl in front of you, and then you one, two, tree, keek! I called it my 'dance of desperation,' but it worked and soon there were conga lines all over the country. Even the Rockefellers are doing eet in Rockefeller Plaza."

In 1938 a New York agent spotted Desi, and next thing he knew, he was the headline attraction in a New York nightclub called La Conga. After he had been there only four months, producer-director George Abbott and Richard Rodgers and Lorenz Hart offered him a lead part in their Broadway show *Too Many Girls*. "Ever acted before?" Mr. Abbott wanted to know.

"Me? All my life!" Desi laughed.

The show opened in Boston, and overnight Desi was a sensation. For the seven months the show ran on Broadway, he was the matinee idol of New York. "And here I am in Hollywood," Desi concluded his life story about three a.m. "Fantasteek, eesn't eet?"

I wasn't surprised; I'd heard this same rags-to-riches story in Hollywood a hundred times. For the old star system wasn't built on talent, or hard work, or acting experience; it was personality that counted. And Desi sure had it.

He enjoyed being the newest male idol but he didn't really believe it. He used to say that he came to this country with nothing, and he'd go with nothing, but at least he'd leave with an extra pair of shoes.

While he had the money, he loved spending it. He roared around Hollywood in a black foreign-made sports car with his initials in gold; beside him sat a succession of movieland's most beautiful single girls — usually blondes: Betty Grable, Gene Tierney, Lana Turner. But more and more, he kept turning up on my doorstep at Ogden Drive, where Grandfather would read him editorials from the *Daily Worker*. Desi was hungry for a family; he'd been rootless for so long.

Everyone at the studio knew I was starry-eyed over Desi, and most of them warned me against him. "He's a flash in the pan," I was told, and, "He's too young for you." Or, "He's a dyed-in-the-wool Catholic and you're Protestant," and so on.

But I had flipped.

*L*ucille in
Dance, Girl, Dance,
the film she was completing
when Desi arrived in
Hollywood, 1940.

C h a p t e r

7

♥

I kept Desi driving up and down the coastline visiting spots I'd seen in my seven years in California, from San Francisco to Tijuana, below the Mexican border. I wanted to share every experience with him, the past included. I even took him to Big Bear Mountain, where we had filmed *Having Wonderful Time*. I was in slacks, shirt, and bandanna; Desi was in an open-necked shirt, tanned the color of mahogany. We looked like a couple of tourists.

Desi ordered a ham-and-cheese sandwich and a beer at Barney's, the local bar-café, and then disappeared to wash his hands. The waitress looked at me and then at Desi's retreating back. "Hey," she said disapprovingly, glancing from my red curls to Desi's blue-black hair, "is he Indian? Because we're not allowed to serve liquor to Indians."

Nobody could picture us as a couple, not even a tourist-hardened waitress.

Too Many Girls was a fun movie to make. Eddie Bracken and Hal LeRoy had been in the original Broadway production along with Desi; Frances Langford, Ann Miller, and I played a trio of coeds. The best of the Rodgers and Hart tunes in the show, "I Didn't Know What Time It Was (Till I Met You)" expressed my feelings about Desi exactly.

"He's another Valentino," the studio bosses predicted. Even the blasé girl extras went around calling Desi "Latin dynamite." Because of Desi's great sex appeal, naturally the RKO bosses wanted to keep him single. His five-year contract, signed before he came to Hollywood, prohibited him from marrying for that length of time.

In September 1940, after the movie was finished, Desi's six-month option was picked up. His RKO contract allowed him half a year on the road, and the same number of months in Hollywood. The author of *Too Many Girls*, George Marion, Jr., was busy writing another Broadway musical in which Desi would star, and RKO had two future movies lined up for him. Meanwhile, the original cast of *Too Many Girls* was opening in Chicago on Labor Day and Desi trained out to join them. I followed in a few days, and we were snapped by the press together at the Pump Room, Desi gazing into a champagne glass and me gazing at him. "She eyes Arnaz," ran the caption.

"You've hit the jackpot at last," a friend at the table told Desi.

"I doubt eet," he replied cheerfully, "but anyway, the best thing that happened to me thees year was meeting Lucille."

Boy, I melted right into his arms. We were criticized for kissing and hugging so much in public, but we were both so gone we didn't care.

I returned to Hollywood to make a movie, and Desi sent me his first telegram, the first of thousands. It was dated October 15, 1940, from Chicago: "Darling, I just got up. I loved your note and adore you. Loads and loads of kisses, Desi."

After *Too Many Girls* closed in Chicago, Desi signed as a headliner with a traveling band. I began making *A Girl, a Guy and a Gob*, which Harold Lloyd produced for RKO. Eric Pommer had hailed me as a "new find," so when Mr. Lloyd asked for me for his picture, the studio bosses said okay. It was a rosy, wonderful time for me. I adored the movie; I had a great time making it.

This was the first Harold Lloyd comedy in which he didn't appear. I played a poor working girl with a screwball family. George Murphy was a sailor and Edmond O'Brien a rich young scion pursuing me. "The lady's family is a little touched," wrote the *New York Times* reviewer. "They play cops and robbers in the parlor, chin themselves in doorways and dance an impromptu conga while Mrs. Leibowitz upstairs gives birth to a son and heir. Lucille Ball may not be made of rubber, but she has as much bounce."

LUCILLE BALL

The *Philadelphia Ledger* said, "A ribticklish comedy . . . Lucille Ball is more sympathetic than she's usually allowed to be." The *Dallas Morning Times* wrote, "Lucille Ball as the daughter of an engaging screwball family handles her task as a romp." The *New York Post:* "Miss Ball has been good for quite some time and now she's better. Bigger pictures than this are calling her."

"Lucille Ball is a dazzling comedienne," another reviewer said. "Beautiful, witty, and with flair. . . . She does a wonderful job of eating an ice cream bar while weeping."

"Darling, I'm in Knoxville," Desi wired me from Tennessee, "and we haven't been able to find a girl to dance with me in the whole town. They haven't even heard of rumbas. I'm so lonesome and bored and worried about that appearance tomorrow."

Then he wired, "Darling, things look swell. I miss you so very much and I'm awfully sorry if I was mean the other night but I love you so much I guess I lost my head. Darling, it was wonderful talking to you tonight but awful when I hung up and was left alone. I'm getting a release from the show and hope to be able to see Palm Springs. Whooppee. Love, Desi."

We saw each other briefly, and then Desi signed for an important appearance at the Versailles nightclub in New York. From there he wired me, "Sweetheart, it is wonderful to know exactly what one wants. These few weeks away from you have been very sad and painful but they have showed me that I want you and you always."

A few days later he wired again from New York: "I'm

so glad you called, Darling. Even if things look bad to you from so far away, please don't make too quick conclusions. I really miss you immensely and am so anxious for you to come to town. So please trust me a little bit, will you? I love you very much."

I knew that Desi had all the debutantes afire again, and pursuing him like crazy. Finally, RKO decided to send me and Maureen O'Hara east to publicize our new movie, *Dance, Girl, Dance*. It bugged me that everywhere we went, Maureen was treated like a lady and I got a stripteaser's reception. An actress gets typed and her real personality is lost in the shuffle.

In Buffalo, my old sidekick from Jamestown High School days, Marion Strong, came to see me and I bubbled and raved about Desi. She had seen me through other love affairs but I had never been so sold on any man before.

Thanksgiving I spent with Desi in New York. We'd been separated for a whole month; again, we couldn't stop talking.

The movie we had made together, *Too Many Girls*, opened at Loew's Criterion and got fine reviews, although Desi's were somewhat mixed. Howard Barnes wrote, "Desi Arnaz is fine as the South American football wonder," but Bosley Crowther wrote rather sourly in the *New York Times*, "Mr. Arnaz is a noisy, black-haired Latin whose face, unfortunately, lacks expression and whose performance is devoid of grace."

Since Desi was packing them in five shows a day at

the Roxy and his appearances at the Versailles were a sellout, he could afford to ignore Mr. Crowther. We had other fish to fry. All we could think and talk about was our future.

One night we sat at a small table at El Morocco and hashed and rehashed our problems. A photographer snapped our picture, and it shows us both staring at the table looking deeply sad and troubled. We discussed the six-year difference in our ages (this bothered only me) and Desi's Catholicism.

Our outlooks on life were very different. Desi's family ranches stretched as far as he could ride a horse in a day. I was raised in a little white house near the railroad tracks and an amusement park; I never even owned a bicycle as a kid. When Desi was fifteen, he was living like a young prince, with cars and speedboats and horses; I was looking for a penny to make subway fare in New York. Desi was raised with the idea that the man's word is law; he makes all the decisions; God made woman only to bear children and run the home.

I wanted a masterful husband, God knows—and part of me wanted to be cherished and cared for. But all my life I'd been taught to be strong and self-reliant and independent, and I wondered if I could change.

We weren't competitive in our careers. Desi's name was as well known in show business as mine and he made just as much money. But he was supposed to spend six months of the year in Hollywood and six months on the road, and what kind of a life was that for us?

Friends kept pointing out that Desi was a romantic. He lived to enjoy life and never thought of tomorrow. I was a levelheaded realist who never lived beyond my means or went overboard drinking or gambling. Nevertheless, I was emotional and sentimental and romantic, too. I was an actress, wasn't I?

I can't do a funny scene unless I believe it. But I can believe wholeheartedly almost any zany scene my writers dream up. No cool-headed realist can do this.

We were both head over heels in love and we both longed with all our hearts for a home of our own and children. But everything else in the picture seemed hopelessly negative; we agreed that night that we could never marry.

The next evening I had to leave New York for a series of personal appearances in the Midwest. In the middle of the night, as the train swayed and rumbled through the hills and valleys of upstate New York, the porter brought me a telegram. It was from Desi. "Just wanted to say I love you, goodnight and be good. I think I'll say I love you again, in fact I will say it. I love you love you love you love you." That was one prop I didn't handle so well. My tears practically turned the telegram to pulp.

I thought everything was over, but Desi couldn't say good-bye. He phoned me almost every hour in Chicago. Then I took a train to Milwaukee, more depressed than I've ever been in my whole life. I had trunkloads of furs and glittering ball gowns with me; I bowed from stages and shook hands and smiled and smiled and smiled. No one guessed my real feelings.

The Milwaukee appearance was for one night at some

kind of benefit they were having. Desi phoned and made me promise to come right back to New York so we could talk some more. But it was now late November and blizzards were arriving in the Midwest. A train carrying Gloria Jean, a starlet who was supposed to follow me at the benefit, got stuck in a snowstorm. The RKO publicity people asked me if I would continue playing in her place. My RKO bosses got on the phone too. They had seen those pictures of me and Desi together in New York and warned me against marrying him. He'd left a trail of broken hearts from Times Square to Sunset Boulevard to East Hampton, they told me. "I'm not going to marry him. Relax," I said. "We both know it's impossible."

My one-day appearance at the Milwaukee benefit stretched into five days. Every evening Desi would phone, hopping mad, and ask when I was leaving for New York. One midnight I came into the hotel after an exhausting day of appearances. Desi was on the phone from New York, so I took the call in the lobby.

"I know now why you're stalling," Desi was yelling into the phone. "There's a verree handsome actor playing een Milwaukee, Joseph Cotten. I suppose there's a beeg theeng between you two — ees that why you're stalling?"

"I don't even know Joseph Cotten," I hollered back at Desi while the whole lobby listened. I'd been so busy working I didn't even know a stage troupe was in town. Just then I looked up and striding through the lobby was — Joseph Cotten. "I'll see you first thing in the morning," I told Desi, and hung up.

I went up to my rooms boiling mad at Desi and told Harriet that I was leaving that minute for New York. She could follow the next day with my clothes. Joseph Cotten was still in the lobby when I came down again and he kindly drove me to the airport. It was then past midnight and there was no regular flight, so I chartered a private plane.

In New York, I checked into the Hampshire House, slept until noon, and then waited for Desi to appear between shows at the Roxy. A woman interviewer arrived just minutes before Desi. I was still mad at him for having so little faith in me, so I let him cool his heels while I went on letting myself be interviewed for an article that wound up with the title "Why I Will Always Remain a Bachelor Girl."

It wasn't until late that night that Desi and I were alone together. He told me why he was so upset about my staying on and on in Milwaukee. He had been arranging an elopement to Greenwich, Connecticut; already he had postponed it five times!

"But I thought we decided that we couldn't get married," I said.

"That's right," he agreed, "but we are."

He left me at my hotel at three a.m., saying he'd pick me up again at eight, and I went to bed deliriously happy. Just before I fell asleep I remembered all my clothes were in Milwaukee with Harriet. All I had was the little black wool number I'd been wearing all day. When I thought about all the appropriately beautiful things I had in my trunk but not available for eight a.m., I was fit to be tied.

But Desi was much too elated to notice his bride wore black. I sat beside him in the back of the car while his business manager drove like sixty over the icy, treacherous winter roads to Greenwich. Desi had a noon show at the Roxy to make.

Inwardly, I was terrified at what I was doing and wondered if I had chosen wisely. Aunt Lola had married a Greek and her life with him was no bed of roses. I knew how Latins can be, how jealous and possessive. But most of all I worried about whether I could make Desi happy.

In many ways, marrying Desi was one of the boldest things I ever did. I had always gone with older men. I had also achieved some kind of stability in Hollywood, and Desi with his beautiful girls and good times seemed headed in another direction.

Yet I sensed in Desi a great need. Beneath that dazzling charm was a homeless boy who had no one to care for him, worry about him, love him. And I wanted him and only him as the father of my children.

All these thoughts drummed through my mind as we tore up the Merritt Parkway to Connecticut. Desi was singing. His dark eyes were shining, his face radiant, but his hands, I noticed, were shaking.

In Greenwich, we spent a harried two hours seeing a judge about waiving the five-day waiting period and getting the necessary health examination. Desi had planned to marry me at the office of Justice of the Peace John J. O'Brien. He had forgotten only one thing: a wedding ring. Desi's business manager ran into Woolworth's and bought me a brass one. Although Desi later gave me a platinum ring, that little discolored brass ring rested among the diamonds and emeralds in my jewel case for years.

At the last moment, the justice of the peace decided that we needed a more romantic spot than his office for the wedding, so he drove us out into the country to the Byram River Beagle Club.

After the short ceremony, we ate our wedding breakfast in front of a bright fire in the club's lounge. Outside, a fresh mantle of snow hung on the pine trees. After all the indecision we'd been through, Desi and I were dazed with happiness. We kissed each other and the marriage certificate again and again. It still has my lipstick marks on it.

"I'm going to keep this forever and ever," I told Desi, clutching it to my black-wool-covered bosom. This marriage had to work. I would do anything, sacrifice anything, to make Desi happy.

Then our intimate little moment together turned into bedlam. Reporters rushed in the doors of the Beagle Club. Desi phoned the manager of the Roxy at 11:55 a.m.

"You're on in five minutes," said Manny calmly, thinking that Desi was in his dressing room at the theater.

"That's what I called you about," said Desi. "I'm een Connecticoot."

"You *can't* be in Connecticut!"

"I know," laughed Desi. "But I am. I been marrying Lucille."

On the car radio driving back to New York we heard the news of our elopement. My mother heard it too, in California. At the stage door of the Roxy we elbowed our way through a mob of cheering fans. Desi carried me over the threshold of his dressing room. Inside we found it packed to the walls with reporters and photographers. Desi led me on the stage, still in that darn old black dress, and thousands of people roared their good wishes and pelted us with rice, thoughtfully supplied by the management.

It was November 30, 1940, the most momentous day of my life so far. I phoned the Hampshire House; Harriet had finally arrived with my clothes. She had been my inseparable companion, at home and on the set, for years. She was flabbergasted. "Who did we marry?" she asked.

In my usual efficient way, I hurried over to the Hampshire House and checked out while Desi celebrated his marriage with some friends in his dressing room. Desi had been staying at the Hotel Maurice with his mother; we decided to begin married life in style at the Pierre. I thought Desi would be delighted to find me all settled there when he finished his last Roxy show that night, but instead he was furious.

"I won't have my wife riding around New York *alone* een a taxi!" he stormed.

I couldn't believe my ears.

"You sure are possessive as hell all of a sudden," I told him.

We glared at each other and then fell helplessly into each other's arms—the way so many of our quarrels were to begin and end for years to come. Friends gave our marriage six months; me, I gave it a week.

I knew that Desi wanted a wife who would play second fiddle to him, and this was all right with me. He wanted to get into the movies and we had big hopes that his exuberant sex appeal, his good taste and intelligence would carry him far—farther than me, I hoped. But his heavy foreign accent limited the roles he could play. Nevertheless, I did everything in my power to advance his career, to bolster his confidence in himself, and to run his home the way he wanted it. This was the way I had been brought up and this was what I wanted.

On our wedding night Desi woke me out of a sound sleep by shaking my shoulders.

"What is it? What's the matter?" I thought the hotel must be on fire.

"I'm thirsty," he explained. "Please get me a glass of water, darling."

I was out of bed and running the tap in the bathroom before I woke up sufficiently to wonder why in the hell he didn't get it himself.

We stayed in New York for six weeks while Desi finished at the Roxy; then I was recalled to Hollywood for retakes on the Harold Lloyd production, *A Girl, a Guy, and a Gob*. On the way back to California on the Super Chief, I began making happy plans for domesticity. I hadn't cooked since my teens in Jamestown and I had no idea what Desi's food tastes were. But whatever they were, I intended to indulge them. As we sat in our compartment ravenously waiting for the dining car to open, I'd say, "What do you feel like eating?"

Then I'd jot down everything in a notebook as he rattled it off—"What's *that?*" "How do you spell it?" "What's in it?" I wrote down God knows what else, wondering if I'd ever get to eat *my* pet dishes, like pot roast and fried chicken. Actually, I'm a Bisquick-variety cook; Desi turned out to be the real chef in the family.

Desi and I were convinced that trying to build a happy marriage right in the heart of Hollywood is very, very difficult. So after we'd been married about six months, we decided to move far out into the open spaces of the San Fernando Valley. It was a blustery, rainy day in March 1941 when we first saw our not-yet-completed little white ranch house in Chatsworth, with a white fence surrounding its five acres. That builder was a good psychologist; the house was just a shell but that fence gave us such a proud sense of ownership. We bought the place for $16,900, and as soon as it was possible to move in, Desi carried me over every threshold and through one window.

Each of us laid the stamp of our different personalities upon that little house. Although it sat on a sandpile when we bought it, I had flowers in profusion before the plumbing was in. I decorated it in Early Victorian and Bastard American; with cabbage-rose wallpaper, red plush chairs, white ruffled curtains, trailing ivy, and beribboned lampshades. I even had some petit point embroidery I'd done as a child in Celoron.

My ideal of womanhood has always been the pioneer woman who fought and worked at her husband's side. She bore the children, kept the home fires burning; she was the hub of the family, the planner and the dreamer.

Desi's idea of family life was based on his childhood in Cuba, where his father owned three ranches, townhouses, an island in Santiago Bay, a racing stable, cars, and speedboats. So the first thing Desi did at our home was hire a bulldozer. He sat on it stripped to the waist, tanned and darkly handsome, glowing with health and vitality, as he dug out a huge swimming pool and then planted groves of orange and lemon trees. Then he built a bathhouse while I adoringly handed him the nails, one by one.

We were so excitingly in love. All my jewelry was marked "To Lucy" on one side, and "Love, Desi" on the other. Around his neck Desi wore a gold Saint Christopher's medal marked "Darling," and he carried a gold lighter engraved: "Dear Desi, my love for you will last longer than this lighter, I betcha, Lucy."

We christened everything in sight Desilu, the combination of our names: the ranch, our station wagon, Desi's first boat, even a special goulash invented by Desi.

Desi was supporting his mother, and I was supporting DeDe and Daddy in the little house on North Ogden Drive; our good friends Bill and Brenda Holden persuaded us that we needed a business manager. I'm a careful spender; Desi is highly extravagant. It would save a lot of arguments, we felt, if we kept our incomes and obligations completely separate.

So right from the beginning of our marriage, our business manager, Andrew Hickox, handled our affairs on this basis. I paid for all my personal expenses, Desi paid for his, and we each contributed a fixed amount every week toward home expenses. Andy gave each of us twenty-five dollars a week for incidentals, and everything else we charged. Andy wrote all the checks and paid the bills from our separate accounts. I was the most cooperative client with money he'd ever known, Andy said, and he's handled many stars. Occasionally I'd go on a clothes spree and then he'd tell me, "Don't spend an unnecessary cent now for the next three months," and I'd do this. I gave him a fixed sum every month to invest, and these holdings have done very well; Desi never was very good at saving.

Once, Desi was playing craps and losing at Vegas. "Let me try," I told him, and took over. Within a short time I won $18,000, and quit. I phoned Andy Hickox and asked him what to do with the pot. "Get a cashier's check for it right away and mail it to me," he said, which I did. When Desi won the same amount of money, he bought a boat.

Having separate accounts works out well in Hollywood. Then when one partner goes on a spending spree, the other can't scream. So although Desi was often extravagant, it was *his* money. As long as he paid half the household expense, he had the perfect right to do whatever he wanted with the rest of it.

It was not
"love at first sight,"
Lucille protested.
"It took five minutes."

Chapter
8
♥

One night soon after we were married, Desi and I had a long, loud fight. The next morning I got out of bed at dawn and walked outside the ranch house. We had a brand-new station wagon parked there. I took a hammer and walked around the new car, smashing every window. What satisfaction that was! Then I telephoned Andy Hickox and told him to get it fixed at my expense.

There isn't that much business managers don't know about their clients. To me, Andy personified cool, impartial judgment. He never took sides in our arguments, since we were both his clients. So one day I phoned Andy and told him to come out to the ranch at eight o'clock that evening.

Desi and I were still at dinner when he came; he joined us for dessert and coffee. "Now let's move into the den," I directed. "Andy, you sit here between Desi and me." We all got settled comfortably and Desi said impatiently, "Okay, Lucy, now what? What's thees all about? How come you asked Andy?"

"We're going to have one of our arguments," I explained calmly to Desi. "And Andy's going to sit here and referee. Okay, let's start."

A complete silence fell. Desi shook his head in bewilderment. Then he started to laugh. Then quiet little Andy broke into guffaws. All three of us sat roaring with laughter. Then Andy said good night and left.

In those early years, our fights were a kind of lovemaking. Desi and I enjoyed them, but they exhausted our friends and family, I'm afraid. Desi even went to Lela Rogers and asked her help in pleasing me. And often I phoned DeDe at three a.m. to recite our latest, loudest, and most passionate fight. DeDe, like our business manager, tried never to take sides, but just the listening, she said, wore her out.

My usual complaint was that Desi only worked at marriage in spurts. I don't believe he ever really intended to settle down and become a good, steady, faithful husband. He said I was much too jealous, and so the arguments roared on and on. But we remained very deeply and passionately in love.

Our rumpus room at the ranch was an early monument to our battles. As Desi once explained to reporter Eleanor Harris, "During that first year of our marriage, every time

LOVE, LUCY

Lucy and I fought, I packed my clothes and moved to a Hollywood hotel. Once there, I unpacked, had my clothes pressed, made up with Lucy, repacked, went home—and had to get my clothes pressed all over again! Repeated endless times, this becomes a highly expensive business; finally, I figured out that it would be a lot cheaper to build myself a glorified doghouse right on our own grounds. Then, after a fight, I could move all my clothes on their hangers from one closet to another. Well, that's how I built our big rumpus house with its main room, bathroom, and kitchen. Grandpa Freddy Hunt helped me shingle the roof. For years, it was our pet place to give parties."

One time, however, Desi announced it was the end of our marriage and he moved in with his mother in her Hollywood apartment. Three miserable days passed and neither of us got in touch with the other. Then one morning at six o'clock I looked out the window and saw Desi standing among the little orange trees he had planted. He was looking about and patting our five dogs on the head at once while tears ran down his cheeks. Once again he was homeless, and uncared for, and he couldn't stand it. Neither could I. I ran bawling out of the house and into his arms.

I'll always remember the first birthday of mine we celebrated in our new little house. It was August 6, 1941, and I was thirty—not an easy birthday for any woman to face.

I thought that Desi had forgotten the day, especially when he sent me off to do some shopping by myself. But at five o'clock, when I drove our station wagon into our long driveway, I found Desi leading a five-piece combo of fellow Latins and forty guests singing "Happy Birthday." The final touch of the romantic, willing spender was the solid carpet of white gardenias floating in our swimming pool.

♥

I loved to bring friends home from the studio. One day I saw a newcomer under the hair dryer at RKO. It was June Havoc's first day on the set and she was unstrung, the tears running down her face as fast as she could wipe them away. "Hey," I told her, pulling back the dryer so she could hear. "I never knew that much water could come out of a human being. How about coming home with me for dinner tonight?" This was the start of an enduring friendship.

Another good friend of mine was Renée DeMarco of the Dancing DeMarcos. I had never even heard of Renée until after I married Desi, and then I learned that he had been engaged to her. They broke up before he came to Hollywood and met me. She married Jody Hutchinson, and after her little daughter was born, she spent a lot of time at the ranch. The biggest disappointment in my life then was not having children. My scrapbooks of my early days in Hollywood — even before I was married — are filled with magazine illustrations of adorable pink-cheeked children. "When?" I'd write next to each picture. "When?" and "When?"

San Fernando Valley was considered the wild and woolly open spaces then, and many movie people built homes there to get away from it all. In the evenings our neighbors would come over to see us—the Bill Holdens, Jack Oakies, Gordon MacRaes, Francis Lederers, Richard Carlsons, and Charlie Ruggleses. We'd play poker or gin rummy, run home movies, or just sit there, feet up, and talk—mostly ranch talk, about when the best time to plant was, which insecticides to use, and how often to irrigate. All that good earthy talk carried me right back to Celoron and my grandfather's livestock and garden. I spent my days at home cooking, hoeing, weeding, washing curtains, and cleaning out closets (a compulsion of mine, since I can't bear to have anything in storage that can be given away).

A few months after Desi and I were married, Carole Lombard and Clark Gable gave us a big, beautiful champagne party at Chasen's in Hollywood. We especially appreciated the gesture since most of our friends were muttering darkly that our marriage wouldn't last six months. Carole often invited us to spend the day at their ranch, which was not far from ours in the San Fernando Valley. Carole and Clark did everything together—they hunted and fished, rode horses and cooked barbecues, and their delight in just being together made a deep and lasting impression on me. This was a marriage. There was only one shadow on their happiness, that I could see. With all her heart, Carole longed to be a mother. She would have made a great one.

More than anything else, Desi and I wanted to costar in a movie together, but we just couldn't persuade the studio bosses that we were an average American couple. I must admit that many of our rows and reunion scenes were public enough;

this may have influenced their opinion of us as a team. Desi kept remembering how enthusiastically the Roxy Theater audience responded when we took a bow together after our elopement. "Let's do a vaudeville act together," he suggested. "If we go over big in Chicago and New York, maybe they'll listen to us in Hollywood."

We opened at the Roxy, playing four or five shows a day, and moved to Brooklyn and Loew's State in Newark. I was glad to exchange the trappings of a glamour queen for baggy pants and a battered derby hat. Desi sang and played the bongo drums; it was a wild, funny act. Soon we had an offer from the Palladium in London. Twice this has happened to us and both times we turned down the offer for the best of reasons: I was pregnant.

We canceled the rest of our bookings and hurried home, mentally planning the nursery addition to our little six-room valley home. On the train ride back to Hollywood, in January 1942, we heard the news of Carole Lombard's death in a plane crash. This tragedy, following so closely upon the heels of Pearl Harbor, was a sickening shock.

Spencer Tracy flew to Nevada to be with The King. He always referred to Clark in this way, half jokingly but in great affection and admiration, too. When Spencer returned, friends asked how Clark was bearing up and if he was drinking much to ease the pain. I'll never forget Spencer's answer: "No drinking. Not for *The King* the easy way out."

During the next few months, we saw Clark tearing around the valley on a motorcycle at top speed. I used to suspect that he was subconsciously trying to kill himself. Clark would come to a screeching stop at our doorstep and come in to talk about Carole by the hour. Sometimes he would bring one of her films over in the evening and we would watch her for a couple of hours. I could never tell whether Clark was deliberately torturing himself, or whether the sight and sound of Carole, so vital and lovely, helped erase at least momentarily the pain of losing her.

During this difficult time for all of us, with the country at war and Carole's tragic death, I lost my baby in the third month of pregnancy. I was sick with disappointment, but confident that things would work out the next time; only, as the months and then years passed, there was no next time.

Desi thought it might divert me and help the war effort to get a few farm animals on the place. He should have known better.

When Desi brought home three hundred baby chicks, I kept them warm in the den at night. When the calf took sick, I moved into the bathhouse with her, covering her with blankets and hot-water bottles. This young spring heifer eventually grew into a large, passionate cow. She used to bawl her head off every time she caught sight of Desi, but the end came when she crashed through our bedroom window to kiss him in bed. We spent close to $1,000 boarding her out one year, since I couldn't bear to sell her.

Our chickens all died of natural causes. We started with the three hundred chicks and three roosters named Saint Francis, Saint George, and Saint John. Finally we had forty superannuated hens and one ancient, blind rooster. Our place became known as the farm for retired chickens. I'd step out the door, call to them, and they'd all hobble over and we'd break into a dance. Everything I did, they did. Or maybe it was vice versa.

I have this rapport with dogs, too, and can carry on quite a conversation. Cats I admire because of their independence. "So you're home again, so who gives a damn?" my cats seem to be saying when I walk in the door.

Naturally I would never allow Desi to touch a hair of the pig we had. I remembered too well those ghastly fall mornings in Celoron when Daddy killed the pig in the backyard.

Desi also put in a huge rotational truck garden which kept twelve families supplied with everything from artichokes to zucchini. Figuring the cost of water, fertilizer, and full-time gardener, I calculated that every last living vegetable cost us about nine dollars per serving. I ate one of our oranges once and it was so sour my mouth turned inside out. We did make a few pennies from our eggs, which I carted into the studio and sold to June Allyson.

We had pretty wild costume parties and other festivities at the ranch. Our spaghetti parties were renowned, with Desi cooking up the sauce, with lots of Spanish herbs, in a big pot.

One night, one of our intimate spaghetti parties grew into fifteen or sixteen people. By seven o'clock, they had long since finished off all my appetizers and gone through every piece of cheese and stale cracker in the house. Desi would come out of the kitchen every few minutes, between stirring and tasting, and announce, "Dinner will be ready pretty soon!"

His sauce was legendary and he would never serve it until it was just right. Finally, as we all sat around the table, napkins tucked in, forks at the ready, he emerged from the kitchen with an enormous casserole pot and announced proudly, *"La comida está lista,"* as the bottom of the pot gave way and the entire spaghetti dinner clumped onto our new cream carpet.

There was frozen silence for a moment or two and then everyone, as if on cue, got up with their plates and forks and bent down to serve themselves off the floor! Cleo still kids me about that hysterically embarrassing night. Thank God I've got friends with a sense of humor.

Word games caused Desi no end of trouble because of his heavy accent. When he was given "Mildred Pierce" in charades, he acted out someone eating and hating it. "But of course," he said later. "Meal-dread!"

Our groups were large and fun-loving. We celebrated Halloween, birthdays, new puppies, salary raises; anything was a pretext for a party. At a Gay Nineties party I wore a fright wig and bloomers and blacked out my front teeth.

At Christmastime, the Francis Lederers would stay overnight since, like us, they had no children. Desi always had musicians out; he's happiest surrounded by Latin rhythms. And presents. He'd have the whole living room stuffed with presents for everyone for miles around. His generosity was legendary. If they ever melted me down, I'd be a pile of gold from his gifts.

While I was alone at the ranch, an accident occurred which later we reproduced almost exactly on the *I Love Lucy* show. I was hurrying out the door one morning when a truck pulled into the driveway with some men who offered to stain the roof shingles with linseed oil and red paint. It seemed like a good idea, so I said okay and left, not even bothering to get their names. But some windows were open and apparently a stiff breeze did the rest. I had just had the whole interior re-upholstered, repainted, and recarpeted, but when I got home that night the entire color scheme was red. The windowsills, the walls, even the cow!

And one of our early parties formed the basis for another *Lucy* show years later. We had asked Marian and Francis Lederer over for dinner along with Renée DeMarco and her new husband, Jody Hutchinson. Someone asked Jody, "How did you meet your wife?" and he told the story in a very romantic, sentimental way. The men thought his tale too slushy for words, but all the women were misty-eyed. Then Francis Lederer spoke up. "Well, it was certainly different with me. I ran and ran until my wife caught me." He kept this kind of banter up until his wife, who is the sweetest, gentlest woman on earth, began to burn. Finally she stood up and announced melodramatically, "You have desecrated my most sacred moment. Lucy, may I stay here overnight?"

I said yes, of course, she certainly could, and this horrified Francis. His wife ran and locked herself in the bathroom. He followed and kept pounding on the door, pleading with her, saying it was all a joke.

The rest of us sat in the living room listening, until Desi said disgustedly, "What's the matter with her? How can an intelligent girl like that act so stupid?"

"Well," I told him heatedly, "he had no right to kid about something like that."

We started bickering and then Renée and her new husband got into a hot argument. The Lederers eventually left arm in arm, happy as larks. Jody and Renée fought all the way home that night (and eventually divorced). Desi and I almost phoned a lawyer then and there.

That night notwithstanding, I was known as a peacemaker in friends' marriage troubles. They told me I had the ability to get down to the essential difference and analyze and set things in perspective. But of course, in my own marriage I found it terribly hard to be objective.

♥

Nothing much seemed to be happening for me at the studio. My $1,000 weekly paycheck came regularly, but I was still a regular among the B's. Then one day Walter Winchell introduced me to Damon Runyon in the commissary and he requested me for the part of Her Highness, the crippled showgirl, in his movie *The Big Street*, with Henry Fonda.

This movie—the biggest hit of my film career—began in the most negative way possible. After Mr. Runyon asked for me, the studio bosses said no, you need a name, and Henry Fonda agreed. He was used to playing with big stars like Margaret Sullavan. But he was under contract to another studio and just owed RKO one picture, so he really didn't give a damn.

It happened that the president of RKO at that moment thought I was good and so I got the part. But the day the shooting was finished, Damon Runyon left RKO, the director joined the Army, and the cutter dropped dead. So the three people who were most responsible for the movie weren't even around when it was edited and cut. In spite of all those handicaps, it was a solid hit, and one of the movies I'm really proud of.

As Charles Laughton once advised me, "If you play a bitch, play it!" *The Big Street* was a light and gay comedy, but like the rest of Damon Runyon's stories, it had its tragic overtones.

Henry Fonda played Little Pinks, a simple, naive busboy who loves Her Highness, a vixenish singer who believes that love "only gives you a one-room apartment, two chins, and a long washline." She becomes incurably crippled and Little Pinks dedicates himself to fulfilling her every whim, including pushing her to Miami in a wheelchair to win a millionaire playboy.

The *New York Herald-Tribune* said, "Lucille Ball gives one of the best portrayals of her career as the ever-grasping, selfish Gloria who takes keen delight in kicking the hapless Little Pinks about."

Life magazine commented, "Lucille Ball's performance is superb—the girl can really act."

Although I got rave reviews, I knew it wasn't going to lead to anything at RKO. I used to discuss my troubles with

a movie exhibitor who was an old friend of mine, Charles Ko-
erner. In 1942, he became president of the studio. He called
me into the front office and said, "Lucy, you're right. They
have no big plans for you around here. For your own good,
you should get up the gumption to leave. A couple of other studios have been asking for you since *The Big Street.* I'll share
your contract with Metro or Paramount. Which do you want?"

I chose MGM because they were tops in musicals. I'd
always had a hankering to be a musical comedy star, probably because I can't seem to do anything well in the musical line.
In August 1942, I signed with Metro for $1,500 a week and
began, in effect, a whole new career.

I knew that RKO was on its last legs financially,
whereas Metro-Goldwyn-Mayer controlled the biggest pool of
creative talent in Hollywood. Louis B. Mayer had more top
actors, writers, directors, and other craftsmen than any other
studio. He earned a salary of half a million dollars a year—
more than any other man in America at that time. His power
and his income were based on his shrewd ability to manipu-
late people for his own productions and for loan-outs and re-
ciprocal deals with other studios. He always loaned his stars
for more money than he was paying them, and the studio pock-
eted the profit.

Mayer regarded every star as having a fixed dollar
value, and his studio was organized into pampering and flat-
tering and manipulating that star to do his bidding. I didn't dig
that too much. When MGM was grooming you, you felt that
you were in the second line of the harem and that in another

twenty minutes they'd be grooming somebody else in your place. And I didn't understand the people too well at MGM, but at least it was all new and different and exciting.

The first day at MGM I was just plain scared. It was a real wrench to leave RKO after seven years, and for the first few months at MGM I had the feeling that some little man was going to tap me on the shoulder and say, "You're wanted back at RKO for retakes." Nobody ever did, and finally I relaxed and put myself into Leo the Lion's masterful hands.

The names on the dressing room doors filled me with awe: Greer Garson, Jessica Tandy, Angela Lansbury, Rosalind Russell, Joan Crawford, Lana Turner, Judy Garland, Esther Williams, and—thank heaven—my old friend at Columbia and RKO, Ann Sothern. The names on the men's dressing rooms were equally celebrated: Jimmy Stewart, Clark Gable, Spencer Tracy, Lionel Barrymore, Mickey Rooney, Hume Cronyn.

I was changed the minute I got over there. Sidney Guilaroff, the hairstylist, had the most to do with it. I had been a redhead at RKO but Sidney changed me to a lighter and more vibrant shade for Technicolor. "Tango Red," he called it, but actually it was as orange as a piece of fruit hanging on a tree. Every time I glanced in a mirror, I reared back, it was so startling. I hated it, but I went along with it. . . . I wouldn't now.

Sidney also changed the style of my hair from long and loose and flowing to up and lacquered, until I had to take the crust off it at night by cracking it with a brush.

The noted designer Irene designed my first stunning suits. The fit and materials were so beautiful. She took me out of frills and gave me tailored, chic things. Irene also introduced me to color in clothes. With my Tango Red hair and blue eyes, she said I was born for Technicolor, so she gave me a flamboyant look to match. I had always stuck to conservative grays, blacks, and beiges (Hattie Carnegie's influence, I guess). Irene put me in colors so vivid I felt like a sunburst, a prism, a tropical bird of paradise. The glowing aqua and tangerine and lime and emerald shades gave me such a gay and lighthearted feeling.

Irene also designed stunning negligees and dressing gowns for me in silks and chiffons, in rosy salmon with lynx collars and emerald satin with marabou.

In *Du Barry Was a Lady,* my first starring role for MGM, they gave me a scarlet, four-cornered mouth and a pastry shop pyramid of orange hair, plus a fifteen-pound white Du Barry pompadour wig. Red Skelton played a nightclub attendant who is slipped a Mickey Finn and awakens to find himself Louis XV. I was the nightclub star he admired from afar, who becomes Madame Du Barry in his dream. Most of the action consisted of Red in satin knee breeches chasing me over and around a big double bed. We practiced for days on a trampoline, which made me acutely seasick.

We all did some spectacular dancing in *Du Barry,* including a very funny bit to the song "Friendship." There was also a dance scene to the hauntingly lovely "Do I Love You?" Cole Porter's songs and Ethel Merman and Bert Lahr had made the show a big hit on Broadway. I made no attempt to copy Ethel Merman's style—she's inimitable—but I was pleased when a New York reviewer commented, "To her red-headed and later bewigged beauty, Miss Ball adds vivaciousness and excellent comedy timing, proving once again that she is a musical-comedy star of the first magnitude."

Getting to know Red Skelton was another plus. I've always thought Red, one of the world's great talents, is basically a very sad clown. And he had this sadness long before he lost his only son to leukemia. Red is an enigma, even, I suspect, to himself. In his most outlandish buffoonery, he makes me cry more than he makes me laugh. Something about him is just inescapably poignant.

Red's house near ours at Palm Springs has an exquisite Japanese garden, on which he lavished some $80,000 worth of imported plants, some of them centuries old. Red himself prunes and trains these trees with fantastic skill and care. On moonlit nights he can be found alone in his teahouse listening to Japanese music and gazing toward San Jacinto Mountain, almost as though he were in Japan and looking at Mount Fuji.

His homes are filled with art treasures and bibelots from all over the world. Yet his tastes are basically so simple that he keeps an electric stove, a pan of water, and some hot dogs by his bedside in case he wakes up and feels hungry.

Red can't even buy a house in a conventional way. He and his artist wife, Georgia, own a twenty-two-room mansion in Beverly Hills crammed with beautiful things, but Red decided that he also wanted a home in the desert. One of his golfing companions at Palm Springs offered to show him his property. So Red went over in his bare feet and bathing trunks to inspect the place. After a brief tour, he said, "Tell you what. I'll buy it for spot cash right now, providing you and your family move out this afternoon." The startled owner was silent as Red calmly pulled $135,000 in loose cash from his bathing trunks. Red shook his hand and the deal was set.

While Red Skelton in satin knee breeches was chasing me around the bedposts in *Du Barry*, Desi was away on a USO tour. I found him only after putting a plea in to the Pentagon to let me know where he was. Desi was also signed at MGM. He was to make a movie called *Bataan*, and got back from the USO tour just in time. *Bataan* was a grim, stark war drama in which thirteen soldiers are picked off, one by one, by the Japanese in the jungle. Desi was cast as Feliz Ramírez, a Spanish-born American soldier who dies of malaria.

When Desi read the shooting script, he realized that during his one big scene, he would be lying under a mosquito net speaking Spanish while Robert Taylor was in front of the camera speaking English.

Desi went to the director, Tay Garnett, and asked if they couldn't at least remove the mosquito netting so audiences could see who he was. Tay agreed, and it was a convincing death scene, but after that, Desi's movie appearances were limited to occasional specialty musical numbers.

From *Du Barry*, I went right into *Best Foot Forward*, with director Edward Buzzell. Eddie gave me my best chance at Metro. He understood my comedy and let me go all out and be my uninhibited self. *Best Foot Forward* was the story of a fading movie star who is invited to a prep school prom. George Abbott directed the New York stage show, which is remembered chiefly for the bouncy tune "Buckle Down, Winsocki." The reviewers found the movie "bubbling, rollicking and charming, sharp and refreshing, with sparkling dialogue and the fresh spirit of youth."

My career at MGM was just getting into high gear when Desi was drafted into the Army in February 1943. One gray morning at dawn I drove him to the railroad station and he joined a group of typical draftees. Desi was hoping to become a bombardier and go overseas; knowing his reckless, impulsive nature and his great patriotism for his adopted country, I never expected to see him alive again. I cried and cried as we said good-bye.

The day he became an American citizen was the proudest in Desi's life. Having lived under a dictatorship, he could really appreciate democracy. Once, when our ranch was seriously threatened by a raging fire, the whole area in the San Fernando Valley roped off, our neighbor Marian Lederer telephoned Desi to ask him what she should save from our house. My jewelry and furs, our sterling silver, and five dogs and six cats were all in danger, but Desi didn't hesitate to answer: "My American citizenship papers!"

In basic training in 1943, Desi broke his kneecap while playing baseball, to his great disgust. He was then assigned to limited service with the Army Medical Corps, entertaining hospitalized servicemen. He was shuttled around to a variety of California army camps, and finally phoned me from Wat-sonville.

"I'm going to be in Birmingham, honey," he said. He sounded very depressed.

"Gee, that's great," I replied. "I'm leaving for a bond tour in the East next week and I'll come to Alabama to see you."

"Birmingham, *California,*" he groaned, naming an army hospital not five miles from the ranch.

At the hospital, Desi did a fine job with the boys back from Bataan and Corregidor and Tarawa. He organized shows and saw that the troops had movies, radios, and books, plus access to all kinds of sports and gym equipment. He helped them with their letters and ordered candy and cigarettes for their rooms. He often put on one-man shows for them playing drums and guitar, and when I could get away, I joined him and we presented our old vaudeville act. Desi was dedicated to these wounded kids and won many commendations for his fine work.

But it galled him not to be overseas himself. He was allowed to leave the hospital every night and weekends, which turned out to be unfortunate. He was too close to Hollywood.

Social life in Hollywood in those days revolved around the studio producers and executives. When Louis B. Mayer deserted his wife in 1944 and moved into Marion Davies's for-mer mansion in Beverly Hills to live high, dozens of other Hollywood bigwigs left *their* wives and followed suit. Mayer and his friends took up gambling, horse racing, yachting, and parties in a big way, and Sergeant Desi went right along with them.

I told Desi that it was all right for some executive or producer in a high financial bracket to join Mr. Mayer in his lively games; they could afford it. But no one approves of an actor enjoying wild parties and late nights; it's too exhausting and shows up immediately in the face and the voice before a camera. I kept telling Desi that these were his bosses and they would have no respect for his reliability and talents as an actor if all they ever saw was a charming, irresponsible playboy.

In 1944, Desi was still under contract to MGM. My dearest hope was that we could costar in a movie after the war. I told movie reporter Gladys Hall, "The only bad feature of this past incredibly wonderful year is that I haven't had Desi. I don't begrudge him to the Service, but I miss him. . . . When Desi comes back, I don't believe there's any doubt but that MGM will realize that in him they have one of the biggest bets in the business. Why, after he made one picture at RKO his fan mail was second only to Ginger Rogers's. And even now, after having been away a year, he still gets two and three hundred fan letters a week."

*T*he master and mistress
of the Desilu Ranch,
in Chatsworth,
California, 1942.

C h a p t e r

9

♥

*D*uring World War II, I was rushed from one extravagant musical to the next with the full star treatment at MGM. This was the heyday of the movies; it was hard to keep a level head and one's sense of values. MGM made overworked, spoiled idols out of Judy Garland, Mickey Rooney, and Elizabeth Taylor; it wasn't the kids' fault, nor the studio's, it was the System. I too was on the spoiling list for a while, but I didn't go along with it.

The studio wanted me to appear at the bosses' parties and entertain them in return. They didn't approve of the "image" I created, living alone at the ranch in dungarees, catering to dogs and cats and my decrepit chickens.

When the day's work was done, I would slip away from the studio as quickly and quietly as I could. The San Fernando Valley was green open spaces then, with rolling horse ranches and walnut and citrus groves. The hour ride to and from the ranch was my "thinking time," the necessary break for reflection.

Desi came home less and less and I was soon caught up in bond tours. A group of us would fly to some city like Philadelphia and make forty-two appearances in a week or ten days. Desi and I communicated more by long-distance than in person.

It was a strange, lonely, unreal kind of life. I clipped out a picture of an adorable baby from a magazine and pasted it along with my movie reviews in my scrapbook. Underneath the baby's smile I wrote, "I don't see any pictures of me in this book and this is your third year of marriage—quit kiddin'!"

In 1943 I made *Meet the People* with Dick Powell. I was a clotheshorse again in this one, a famous actress who becomes a welder in a factory "to meet the people." It wasn't a good movie but I enjoyed working with Dick. He was a great natural performer. He was so natural that he was not always given the credit he deserved. Dick didn't make noise about his acting, or his marriage troubles, or even his losing fight with cancer. A sane, sensible, stoic man, he was also a loving husband and father and a showman of rare ability.

In January 1944, my grandfather Freddy, my beloved Daddy, died of a stroke at seventy-eight. We never even considered burying him in Hollywood; he belonged next to Flora

Belle in the elm-shaded Hunt family plot in Jamestown. I flew east for his funeral and then stayed at the Jamestown Hotel for several days, seeing old friends and helping raise money for a war bond drive.

I told local newspapermen that Desi was still the number-one interest in my life and that I hoped to costar in a picture with him after the war. Telephone calls and telegrams from Desi flooded the hotel during my four-day stay, and everyone assumed we were still honeymooning. Then I returned to Hollywood to make *Ziegfeld Follies*.

This was a great, glittering, lavish production of Arthur Freed's, with many top stars, including Fred Astaire, Judy Garland, Lena Horne, and Gene Kelly. I was promised that I could dance with Fred Astaire and do some Bea Lillie–type sketches. But it was such a stupendous production, involving so many egos and temperaments, that I ended up doing nothing but cracking a rhinestone-studded whip over eight black panthers. *Ziegfeld Follies* got terrible reviews; it was a costly dud, lacking all sparkle and originality.

Once again I learned the bitter lesson that directors and producers can make or break an actress. I was a star, but I felt that I couldn't afford to turn down parts for fear of infuriating these bigwigs—"Who does she think *she* is, putting her judgment above ours?" If I did turn down a script (which I never did while under contract), I would be put on suspension, without salary. I couldn't accept an offer from any other studio, no matter how good, yet I could be fired at any time without the bosses showing cause. In some ways, it was wonderful to be a contract player under the wing of a powerful studio, but at the same time it was a master-serf relationship. All the glittering "stars" were at the mercy of the whims of the top people. The studio executives and producers were the *in* group; the writers and actors and directors were the *out* group. The major war was between the *in* and the *out* groups, but equally savage wars raged within.

I knew I had the *ability,* and I set myself to learn a difficult and demanding craft with as much self-discipline as I could muster. Most people at RKO and MGM knew I had something, but nobody knew quite what. They made the mistake of giving me gags, whereas I find my comedy is in the tradition of pure physical comedy. I must be given a comic situation which I live with, tussle with; then the twists and complications emerge.

At MGM during the war years, the producers were always in love with a different girl every day of the week, and some of the things that were planned for me were given to other actresses. I didn't particularly care. My tiny part in *Ziegfeld Follies* was a disappointment, but I went on to play a supporting role in *Without Love,* starring Katharine Hepburn and Spencer Tracy.

It was tremendously exciting to be in a picture with Hepburn, whom I had admired so much at RKO. Katie seemed to lead a lonely life, but she is probably the least lonely woman I know. She is also one of those rare persons secure enough to disregard convention and yet retain her sense of dedication and self-respect.

Spencer Tracy is a brooding, strange man with a great

depth of feeling for those close to him. In his leisure moments, Spence is relaxed and can be extremely entertaining. On the set, he is all business. When you're working with Spencer, you don't kid around.

Without Love was based on the Philip Barry play about a young widow who wants to keep bright the memory of a perfect marriage, and a love-weary scientist who is marriage-shy. In my supporting role, Bosley Crowther noted, "Lucille Ball throws wisecracks like baseballs."

While I was knocking myself out with moviemaking and bond tours, my marriage was crashing fast. Desi's nightlife had even blasé Hollywood talking. *Confidential* magazine published a story about a Palm Springs weekend of his, and this too hurt and humiliated me deeply. At a Birmingham Hospital picnic that summer, Desi got roaring drunk and called his superior officer some pretty unprintable names. I was sure he'd be busted from sergeant to private, but because he was doing such a fine job with the wounded men, he was let off with a reprimand. Desi never could accept authority easily.

During the summer of 1944, Desi stopped coming home. One night I tossed sleeplessly until dawn wondering where our marriage had gone awry and what I had done wrong.

Finally I hit upon a desperate measure. I still loved Desi; he was the only man in my life. But I decided to divorce him. I chose California because a divorce there takes a year to become final, and therefore there were 365 days left for a reconciliation.

Cleo was married and living in an army camp in North

Carolina, and DeDe was visiting her there. I telephoned them to say that I was divorcing Desi. "It's too bad you can't work things out," Cleo commented. "You two have so much going for you."

"I know that," I agreed. "But now Desi's even blaming me for the war."

The night before I was scheduled to make my appearance in court, Desi showed up. He was contrite, and his most charming self. The next morning I climbed out of our big double bed and started to put on a suit, picture hat, and jewelry. "Where're you going?" Desi wanted to know.

"To court, to divorce you," I told him.

I told the judge that Desi had caused me "grievous mental suffering."

I didn't expect Desi to be around when I got back to the ranch later that morning, but he was. He looked white and stricken. "Lucy," he said, "the next time I marry, I'm going to be a better husband."

"And the next time I marry, I'm going to be a better wife," I answered truthfully.

Desi's face brightened. "Then why don't we both try it on each other?" he suggested.

I didn't believe Desi could change, but he did for a time. I gulped a bit when I paid $2,000 in fees for the divorce I never got, but it was worth it.

For a long time, Desi came home every night and we both tried very hard to make things work. I no longer expected to be as happy as I had been as an ecstatic new bride, but I did look for a measure of peace and security.

I closed my eyes, put blinders on, and ignored what was too painful to think about. I tried to view my troubles less seriously, and worry less. I tried to curb my temper. Things said in embarrassment and anger are seldom the truth, but are said to hurt and wound the other person. Once said, they can never be taken back.

During this period of reconciliation, a reporter asked Desi what adjustment he had contributed to our marriage. He fell into a prolonged silence, then finally came up with two: "Well, I try to sleep with the damn windows open because Lucy likes fresh air. Then I took up square dancing for a while; I went around jumping with the rest of the characters!"

Around this time, my good friend director Eddie Buzzell asked for me for his picture *Easy to Wed*. This was a remake of an early Jean Harlow movie, *Libeled Lady*, and one of the highlights of my movie career.

The plot concerned a rich playgirl (Esther Williams) who sues a newspaper for a libelous story about her. The paper hires a great lover (Van Johnson) to compromise her so that the suit will be forgotten. I played a showgirl again, in ringlets, black tights, and short bustle, but instead of being the hard-boiled type with all the answers, I was an unsophisticated poor soul—a chorus girl who was being used and stepped on and was fighting back in her own way.

Eddie Buzzell put me at my ease, and encouraged me to be myself in a way no other director had done before. I was sick and tired of "drop gag" parts where I strolled through a room, dropped an acidly humorous remark, and left.

Eddie, who came to Hollywood through the Orpheum

vaudeville circuit, used to attend our parties at the ranch. He had seen me do my silly chicken dance with our flock of ancient hens. He saw the potential in me for humor and pathos I didn't even know I had.

I had a driving, consuming ambition to succeed in show business but I had no idea where my real talents lay. I was dying to be told, to be shown. Way down deep underneath those brassy showgirl trappings was Lucy, and there she stayed, strangulated, for years.

Easy to Wed was released to sterling reviews. After knocking myself out, giving my best possible performance in this picture, I expected other good roles to follow. Instead, I was put into a real dog with John Hodiak called *Two Smart People.* At least the critics knew how to call it.

The *New York Times* described *Two Smart People* as "a dog-eared tale about love and the confidence racket. Lucille Ball plays the beauteous dame who falls for the guy she started out to fleece. She is painfully defeated by the script at every turn. But in addition to its pedestrian plot, *Two Smart People* suffers from a lack of competent direction."

In November 1945, Desi was released from the Army and hurried home to take up his interrupted movie career. He hoped to have an excellent part in a movie called *Fiesta,* but MGM had been grooming Ricardo Montalban in Desi's absence and gave it to him instead.

We talked long and seriously about what Desi should do. Since nothing seemed cooking in the movies for him, he turned to his next love: music. He asked for his release from MGM and started to put together a rumba band.

Nothing seemed to be working out for either of us. My movie career seemed just as stalled at MGM as it had been at RKO. I was making $3,500 a week, but I wasn't getting anywhere. The years were speeding by—I was still childless and my dream of co-starring with Desi and working side by side as a team seemed hopeless.

Whenever I could, I went to Desi's nightclub openings, but I didn't enjoy them much. If I watched him too closely, I was accused of being there "to keep an eye on him"; if I didn't appear, I was taunted with concentrating too much on my own career.

♥

I blame a lot of my troubles at MGM on the agent I had at that time. Now, I had always been aware that until you get to a certain point in your career, no agent can help you; you have to advance yourself. By this time, however, at $3,500 weekly I was near the top of the heap financially. But I soon learned that my agent had little regard for me as a person or a performer, and when the chips were down, he was not on my side.

All my affairs were being handled by this agent, and I wanted to have a serious discussion with him about what I was doing, what was going to further my career, what kinds of roles were good or bad for me. But he couldn't be bothered, and next thing I knew, I had been loaned out to a totally strange studio without my consent or even my knowledge. The movie was *The Dark Corner* for 20th Century-Fox, with Mark Stevens, Clifton Webb, and William Bendix. Twentieth

Century was paying $6,000 a week for my services, but I got only a portion of this; MGM and my agent pocketed the difference. This in itself infuriated me.

On my first day of work, Harriet and I drove to the 20th Century studios. We passed a place near our ranch where a ragged mongrel pup was chained up. I'm kind of a nut on the subject of cruelty to animals; I was upset to see this dog chained in the hot sun without shelter or water. He raced back and forth in a frenzied desperation as we drove by, almost breaking his neck.

Harriet noticed that I turned very white and began to tremble. For some reason, that lonely pup really got to me that day. The experience left me oddly off balance.

Looking back, I think I must have been going through a mild nervous breakdown at this time. On the weekends, Desi would sit beside the pool most of the day, depressed and miserable. "Look at him!" I'd tell DeDe. "Brooding again!"

"It's not good for a man when the woman's the breadwinner of the family," DeDe replied calmly. What could I say? I believed this too.

My brother Freddy and cousin Cleo were having difficulties around this time and DeDe accused me of helping them too much. "You're so strong that you do too much for those you love," she scolded me. "That weakens them and lets them slide."

I was trying to be a good trouper, a good neighbor, and sister and wife. I was trying as hard as I could, but everything seemed to be going wrong and everyone was blaming me.

When I fluffed my lines on the set the next week and the director said sharply, "Lucy, have you been drinking?" I'd never in my life been accused of such a ridiculous thing. I needed sympathy, understanding, help, but was met only with coldness and hostility. I complained to my agent, "I don't know what's happening on that set, but they're accusing me of all kinds of things."

He replied coldly, "Well, from what I hear, what *are* you doing?"

Well, that's all I needed, so I said, "Why don't you come on the set and see if I don't know my lines or if I'm wasting time."

So that day my agent bothered to show up, but it was too late. I was so unstrung I couldn't get a word out. I'd never had any trouble with my work before, and to be suddenly called a slacker was more than I could take. "I want Marc, I want Marc," I cried, over and over. I wanted Marc Rabwin. Dr. Rabwin was not only my doctor and one of the finest surgeons in the country, he was my mentor, my friend. I needed someone who would come and help me. So by this time, everyone on the set was alarmed and they phoned Marc and DeDe, and they both came over and took me home.

This was highly unusual behavior for me; I've never forgotten that moment. Today if anyone gets unpleasant with me on the set, I say, "Hey, what is *that?* If I've done something wrong, let's deal with it directly. Don't be snide or sarcastic." And I try to remain sensitive to others' feelings on the set. You never know what else people are dealing with in their lives and how those pressures might be affecting their performance.

But of course, I'm in a different position now. They only pick on you when you can be picked on. After you reach a certain level, they wouldn't dare treat you so rudely.

As for my own mini-breakdown, I realize now that I had been trying to embrace too much, taking on too many burdens—emotional and financial. As a result, I was exhausted, just completely depleted in every way. This made me unsure of myself and unstrung. I had enough technical skill to turn in a good performance regardless, and *The Dark Corner* was hailed as "tough-fibered, exciting entertainment," with "superior performances." I can't say my performance was superior; I look utterly bemused in this movie, with a staring, numb, fogbank look, as if *I* were being driven into a dark corner.

I was a very sick girl for three months afterward. I was having a terrible time with Desi, and my agent had me sewn up so tight that the only way I could get him out of my life was to leave MGM. I regretted this keenly but it was the only legal way in which I could get rid of that agent's representation. Afterward, I swore I would never again be "packaged out" to anybody without my say-so, and I never was.

The day I left MGM, I went up to Louis B. Mayer's impressive front office to say good-bye. The movie industry's most powerful tycoon was still living it up and our paths rarely crossed outside the studio gates. He said he was very sorry to see me go.

I said good-bye to my friends on the lot and left the

studio for good, I thought. I was terribly depressed. Life seemed unbearable. Desi was away rounding up a new band, so I sat home alone and cried. I was still stuttering, and this terrified me.

Then one day Kurt Frings, a well-known agent, drove the twenty-five miles out from Hollywood to our ranch to see me. He told me that Olivia De Havilland had sent him. She had heard about my difficulties and thought perhaps he could help me. I hardly knew Olivia except to say hello. I was bowled over by her kindness.

Olivia De Havilland had been involved in the same kind of "package" dealing with the same agent that had been representing me. She had refused roles and had been put on suspension. Olivia fought a bitter eighteen-month court battle with the agent and won. Because she courageously fought the System, we all benefited.

Kurt Frings suggested that I free-lance, and in fact, he had a picture all ready for me at Universal. "I can't, I can't," I told him. "All I do is stut-stut-stutter."

Frings kept talking to me, quietly and soothingly, and almost persuaded me to do *Lover Come Back* with George Brent. Then the director, Bill Seiter, called and said, "You're a great gal. . . . We need you. . . . Come on over to Universal and go to work."

"I c-c-can't read a l-l-line," I told him.

Bill said, "Of course you can." I went over to Universal and he laughed at me for three days while I stuttered. By the fifth day I was talking with no difficulty. *Lover Come Back* got poor reviews, but it saved me. Howard Barnes of the *New York Herald-Tribune* wrote, "Our sympathy to Miss Ball, who is fetching in Travis Banton's gowns in spite of the plot's ennui." Bosley Crowther said, "Miss Ball wears a wardrobe of costumes and acts as if she really had a script. The poor lady is sadly deluded, she is completely without support."

But although the scriptwriters were viewed to have failed me, the director and other players did not. Making *Lover Come Back* was the best thing I could have done. I will never forget the understanding and help Bill Seiter gave me when I needed it most. I will always be grateful. And George Brent was a wonderfully supportive co-star.

While I was making *Lover Come Back* in the spring of 1946, Desi and his band opened to enthusiastic reviews at Ciro's. His next engagement was at the Copacabana in New York. For the first time in eleven years, I was not under contract to a studio and was free to take an extended vacation. I took six months off; Desi and I boarded a train for New York, along with Harriet and Desi's sixteen band members.

We took a big apartment at the Delmonico Hotel at Fifty-ninth Street and Park Avenue. Desi and I had a ball. He had to play at the Copa most of the night and liked to sleep until noon. When I got up at my usual early hour, I'd lock the bedroom door so the hotel maids wouldn't go in and disturb him. One day DeDe phoned me from California and said, "What's this I read in Sheilah Graham's column? It says here you lock Desi out of the bedroom and he pounds on the door and shouts and hollers."

"Whaat?" I said. "That's a pack of lies!"

I called Sheilah Graham hopping mad and demanded a retraction.

"Lucy, I wouldn't write something like that unless it came on good authority!"

She finally admitted that someone in the hotel had tipped her off. Then I figured out how it all started. It was summertime and our bedroom was on an inner court, with the windows open. Harriet and I would often go shopping in the morning, and once when we got back Desi was awake, banging on the locked bedroom door and yelling, "Lucy! Lucy! The door's locked!"

Somebody on the court heard this and reported it to Sheilah, who printed it without checking. She's never forgotten how furious I was. But Desi and I were so happily reconciled that I wanted nothing to spoil it, least of all an incorrect item in a gossip column.

This year, 1946, was the movies' peak year, when some ninety million people went to the movies every week. It was also the year that five of my movies were playing on Broadway at the same time. When I lunched with old friends at Mamma Leone's, I was mobbed by fans with autograph books. It was my first experience being a New York celebrity and I found it unsettling, especially when hordes of teenagers with pads and pencils sprang out at me everywhere.

"The little . . . uh . . . rascals are a menace," I remarked to a reporter, diving into a one a.m. breakfast at "21."

The reporter asked me about my experience making

The Dark Corner, which was being premiered that day. "What's it all about?" I asked the interviewer. "Honestly, I have no idea what the story is. Most of my scenes were with Mark Stevens and I never did know what the rest of the people were doing. I guess I'll have to go see it." I could almost hear the 20th Century press agent grinding his teeth, and I chuckled inwardly. I hoped that the movie which gave me such trouble would be a bomb; actually it did quite well.

The only picture of the five on Broadway I really cared about was *Easy to Wed,* the comedy I did with Eddie Buzzell at MGM. I went to see this with musical comedy star Jane Kean, who was then appearing in the Broadway show *Are You with It?*

I had only just met the attractive and vivacious Jane, but liked her immediately. "It's such a pleasure to know you, Miss Ball," she said very formally when we were introduced.

"Well, you'll know me all my life," I answered. Jane and I have been close ever since.

The day we went to see *Easy to Wed* at the Palace in New York, there was a long line of people waiting. I had just come from dining with Desi at the Copacabana and was wearing a cocktail dress and a Lilly Daché hat of turquoise feathers. When Jane and I got out of the cab, I joined the end of the line on Fiftieth Street, three blocks from the theater.

Jane was amazed. "You're the star of this movie. Why don't you see the manager and he'll let you right in?" she suggested.

"Oh, I don't want to do *that,*" I told her. "Supposing I say, 'I'm Lucille Ball,' and he says, 'So what?'"

Jane looked at me and shook her head. "And to think I took you for a domineering female."

Finally Jane went into the theater, and fortunately the manager laid down the red carpet for both of us. I guess I couldn't forget all my abortive attempts to get into a vaudeville act on that same Palace stage, back in my early days in New York.

While I was vacationing in New York, I was invited to Jamestown to help raise money for the Little Theater. The town fathers asked me what kind of a benefit party I'd like and I suggested a boat ride on the SS *City of Jamestown* to Chautauqua.

I didn't realize that they'd have to raise the old steamboat from the bottom of the lake. But they did, and then during the ride every time I'd move from port to starboard to enjoy another familiar view of the lake, everyone on board would follow me and the boat would list dangerously low on that side. The captain kept saying, "Everybody stay in the middle of the boat!" But it was a beautiful moonlit trip.

"There's no other place in the world like Jamestown," I told the local reporter. "They'll tell you that California is God's country, but God's country is right here in Jamestown. I can't possibly tell you how much this place means to me, because of the normal, happy childhood it gave me and offers to every youngster."

The only thing that disturbed me about the visit was that some of my old friends didn't show up. They were timid about meeting a "movie star." When they did see me, they jumped to the other side of the street in confusion. And a few stood there with a big chip on their shoulder, waiting for me to knock it off. I finally put an ad in the paper, asking my old friends to stop by the hotel. But it took another ten years for me to have a real homecoming in Jamestown.

*Crossing the Roxy
threshold again,
ten years later.*

Chapter

1 0

♥

Our New York idyll couldn't last forever. Desi got pretty busy. He made *Cuban Pete* for Universal in 1946. He was also musical director for Bob Hope's radio show, and the rest of the time he toured the United States and Canada. Desi was well acquainted with performing in the best nightspots in New York and Miami; now he learned how people reacted to his showmanship in Kalamazoo and Chagrin Falls. He was well liked wherever he went, and clubs and theaters were always happy to have him back.

Other bandleaders respected his talents and knew that he ran a well-paid outfit. Even if he ended up with nothing after a particular engagement, Desi always saw that his boys were taken care of. At Vegas, Desi made the most money but generally left it behind. One night he dropped $48,000 at the gambling tables. But as we'd established from the first days of our marriage, his finances were his own business. He ran his band in his own way, and in a few years he was netting $2,500 a week.

Desi eventually got sick of running around the country for one-night stands, but he never got sick of leading a band. Because he *loves* music. When he sits at the bongo drums pounding out those pulse-racing rhythms, his smile is ecstatic, his great dark eyes glow. That's when he's happiest.

That said, starting a band from scratch and trying to build a national reputation isn't easy. During the first year, when money was pretty tight, several of his musicians fell ill and had to be hospitalized. Desi could have replaced the sick men with other players and continued on his tour. Instead, he canceled several engagements and dug deep into his reserve funds to pay both his idle musicians and a pile of medical bills.

While Desi was on the road, I hired a tutor and studied literature and languages three nights a week. I made *My Awful Wife* and *Her Husband's Affairs* for Columbia with Franchot Tone, and *Lured* for United Artists. In *Lured*, a routine whodunit, I played a taxi dancer in London who is used as criminal bait by Scotland Yard. George Sanders played opposite me, and Charles Coburn and Sir Cedric Hardwicke had supporting roles.

Around this time, June Havoc was staying with us at

the ranch. She's such a bright, warm, fun-loving person, who I thoroughly enjoy having around. One day she said to me, "Lucy, I know you're going stir-crazy! Why don't you take a big chunk of time—now that Desi's away and you're free-lancing—and tour the country with a play?"

Soon afterward, two producers who were running the Princeton Drama Festival that summer talked me into doing *Dream Girl.* Havoc (as we all referred to her) had appeared in this Elmer Rice play on Broadway and she thought it would be a good vehicle for me. It was the first chance I'd had in years to get away from Hollywood, and of course, to me, the stage had always been "it."

We opened in Princeton's McCarter Theatre in June 1947, and ended up touring the whole country, big towns and small, for twenty-seven weeks, or almost seven months, much longer than I had expected. *Dream Girl* was a *tour de force* written especially for Betty Field—who was great in it—but it gave me a chance to demonstrate some versatility, a chance Hollywood kept denying me. The reviews were warm and welcoming.

One night, two gentlemen came backstage and introduced themselves as my former teachers at the John Murray Anderson dramatic school in New York. They congratulated me warmly on my performance and said that they had recognized my potential years ago. That gave me a chuckle, but I was pleased, too. I didn't take the opportunity to remind them that I'd been kicked out of their school for lack of talent.

During my tour, Desi's busload of musicians had a terrible accident near La Porte, Indiana, when the bus driver fell asleep at the wheel at eighty-five miles an hour. One of the boys lost an eye and some of the others were badly cut up. My brother Freddy was their band manager, and both he and Desi narrowly missed being killed, because they had decided to charter a plane to catch me in *Dream Girl* in Detroit that day. Fate was certainly looking out for them, because only six men of the sixteen-piece orchestra were unhurt. The two who took over Desi's and Freddy's regular seats up front were hurt the worst. One of them, Charlie Harris, broke many bones and he was the one who lost an eye.

Desi immediately flew back to join the band. They had a date to keep that night in Akron, Ohio, and a cancellation would have cost him dearly. But news of the accident spread and half a dozen competing bands came to Desi's rescue. They sent a pianist, a whole trumpet section, drummers, and maraca players to Akron to replace the injured musicians. Desi never forgot that. "Helping the fellow who's in a tough spot is the best thing about America," he always said.

On January 6, 1948, we brought *Dream Girl* to Los Angeles, after performances in Boston, Detroit, Milwaukee, and many other cities. It was expensive to bring the large cast and the scenery from the East Coast; I wound up contributing to the move to Hollywood for the sake of our cast's newer actors, kids who wanted to be seen where it might count.

The show ended in Los Angeles after most of the cast was felled by a terrible virus—including me.

In 1948, the movie industry was in a panic. The year

before, MGM had gone $6,500,000 into the red. Now budgets were being slashed and the number of contract players cut in half, and the spate of productions dwindled to a trickle. All over the country, movie theaters were closing, as customers went elsewhere or stayed home with the radio and a new threat, television.

Like many of my colleagues, I began to cast a speculative eye toward radio. Back in 1946, Hubbell Robinson of CBS, vice president in charge of programming, had talked to me about a domestic comedy show based upon the book *Mr. and Mrs. Cugat.* I was interested, especially if Desi could costar, but the big brass at CBS thought he was not the type to play a typical American husband. "But he *is* my husband," I told them, "and I think it helps make a domestic comedy more believable when the audience knows the couple are actually married."

I knew, too, that radio interfered less with a normal home life than any other entertainment medium, a fact borne out by the experiences of such happily married radio greats as Mary Livingstone and Jack Benny, Fred Allen and Portland Hoffa, Gracie Allen and George Burns, and Harriet and Ozzie Nelson.

But CBS turned a deaf ear to my proposal to team me up with Desi. So finally I relented and did a series with Richard Denning called *My Favorite Husband,* based on the Cugat book.

This half-hour weekly show was similar to *I Love Lucy* only in that I played a wacky wife. I was married to the fifth vice president of a bank and trying in comic ways to promote his career. Gale Gordon was the bank president—the same role that was to be his on *The Lucy Show.* I found radio a wonderful way to make a lot of extra money. It was easy because although we had a studio audience, I could read the script. I didn't have to memorize it. If I was busy on a movie set during the day, we'd rehearse and tape at night. Radio was very big then in Hollywood and everyone in the movie industry was getting into it.

My writers on *My Favorite Husband* were Madelyn Pugh, Bob Carroll, Jr., and producer-director Jess Oppenheimer, a connection that would become particularly fruitful in years to come. Jess Oppenheimer had written for several radio stars, including Jack Benny, Edgar Bergen, and Fanny Brice. He assured me that the audiences would laugh if I looked directly at them, rather than down at the words. I didn't believe him until he sent me to see a Jack Benny show. For the first time, I realized how Jack could make a funny remark and then, simply by gazing deadpan at the audience, sustain the laughter another forty-five seconds. Our commercial sponsor, Jell-O, wanted me to do some funny nursery rhyme commercials at the end of the program, and taking my cue from Jack Benny, I began to mug, use my body, and turn directly to the audience. It worked.

In 1949, Desi and I instituted a "stay at home" policy. I was still childless, which caused me great heartache. Freddy and Cleo were both married and had kids of their own; I had dogs and cats. So one day, Desi and I sat in our cabbage-rose-papered living room and talked far into the night. We finally decided that Desi would give up his cross-country tours and only take local engagements with his band. We would both consult doctors to see why we did not have children.

And we would "kick out the bums." Desi had many hangers-on at our ranch at this time. Drinking, brawling, constantly dropping in, they gave us no peace. We had to take over our own home again, losing the parasites for good.

I told Desi that I would try to be a better wife, more loving, more understanding. To prove that I really meant to make a major effort, I started taking instruction in the Catholic faith. I thought that because Desi and I had eloped and had been married by a judge, our marriage somehow lacked a certain sacred quality. So we were married again in 1949 in Our Lady of the Valley Church in Canoga Park. Groucho Marx couldn't make the ceremony, but he wired: "What's new?"

Desi and his band were appearing on Hollywood's Sunset Strip the June day we remarried. He wore a white suit and I was in a blue satin wedding dress with a bridal bouquet. My mentor in comedy techniques, Ed Sedgwick, gave me away and Desi's mother, Dolores, was matron of honor. I thought it would please her to have us married in the Church, and I promised to bring up any children we might have as Catholics.

It was a sentimental occasion, with our closest friends and family there, and a wedding reception afterward. It was a beautiful ceremony, and I believed in it. At the time, I seriously intended to become a Catholic. I took instruction for a long time, but lost the inspiration when I realized that Catholicism did not seem to help Desi in his life.

In 1949, I signed a contract with Columbia for one picture a year. Desi did a picture for Columbia that same year called *Holiday in Havana,* and was still Bob Hope's musical director on his radio show. His band was now so successful that he was getting $12,000 a week for appearances, and I was very proud of him.

This year was the beginning of my great association with Bob Hope. We did *Sorrowful Jones* together, a remake of the Damon Runyon story *Little Miss Marker* which originally starred Shirley Temple. Going to Bob's set every day was like going to a party; I couldn't wait to get there. And I loved working with him.

Bob is predictable and never moody. He's fun, sweet, kind, good; a gentleman and a trouper. I can bounce vitriolic remarks off his big chest and they come out funny, not like acid. Because he's such a strong male figure, he makes me appear more feminine.

Like everything Damon Runyon wrote, *Sorrowful Jones* had pathos as well as comedy, and Bob at first was rather afraid of the straight scenes. "What if the audience laughs in the wrong place?" he worried. He was feeling his way, and so was I. And this was the first movie I'd ever made with Bob. But after a few days, when he still seemed a bit uneasy, I found the courage to take him aside and say, "Don't be afraid to play it straight. If *you* believe in the scene, the audience will, too."

We started shooting and everything went along great, except that a horse stepped on my foot during one scene and hurt my toes so badly I've been wearing open-toed shoes ever since.

In 1949, I also made *Miss Grant Takes Richmond*, with Bill Holden, and then, in August, a second film with Bob Hope, *Fancy Pants*. By this time I had "arrived" in Hollywood to the extent that directors and producers spoke of "a Lucille Ball–type role" when casting their pictures.

When I made *The Fuller Brush Girl*, however, in March 1950, I began to wonder just how much I wanted to play that Ball role. We got great reviews and the bits were quite funny, but what I remember this movie for chiefly is the truly terrible migraine headaches I suffered making it. And no wonder! In filming all this wild slapstick, I sprained both wrists and displaced six vertebrae, then irritated my sciatic nerve by walking on the outside of my ankles for hours doing a drunk scene. I also suffered a two-day paralysis of the eyeball when talcum powder was accidentally blown into my eye by a wind machine. A three-day dunking in a wine vat gave me a severe cold, and I also was bruised by several tons of coffee beans. At any rate, at five o'clock on the last day of shooting, I was climbing into my car to drive directly home to bed, when I remembered that I had promised to pose for publicity shots for the local tuberculosis society.

So I drove to Hollywood and Vine. Coughing and sneezing, I stood in front of the free chest X-ray machine they had set up there. The technician developed the film in a couple of seconds. "Pardon me, Miss Ball," he gasped, "but this X ray shows that you have some kind of pneumonia."

"I do?" I said. "I thought I just had a cold." I drove

right to the hospital and spent the next nine days in the thermostatic pneumonia wagon.

♥

One spring day in 1950, Desi and I decided that since nobody else seemed to have faith in us as a team, we'd form our own corporation to promote ourselves. We had our manager constitute our partnership legally. Desilu Productions, Inc., was launched.

It was important to find out how the public reacted to us together, so with the help of Pepito Pérez, the renowned Spanish clown, and my radio writers, we put together a Mr. and Mrs. Vaudeville act. Desi sang and played the bongo drums; I kept trying to butt into his nightclub act. I also did a baggy-pants routine with a cello loaded with a stool, a plunger, flowers, and other props, and flipped and barked like a seal. That hour-long act was a real potpourri of all our talents — like one of our Desilu goulash parties at the ranch.

We broke the act in around San Diego and San Francisco at various army camps. When word got around that we were liked, six months' worth of theater contracts materialized throughout the U.S.A. and at the Palladium in London. During a miserably hot week in June 1950, we flew the troupe into Chicago. Desi and I spent the afternoon rehearsing and then went to dinner at the Pump Room, returning to our hotel room about midnight. As I climbed into bed, I noticed sleepily that some of the bureau drawers were half open and their contents were spilling out. "Why did Harriet leave everything in such a mess?" I wondered as I fell asleep.

L O V E ,   L U C Y

At four a.m., I woke up, sat bolt upright in bed, and exclaimed, "Harriet would never do a thing like that!" I switched on the lights and cried out: "Desi, we've been robbed!"

All my jewelry was gone, including the forty-carat aquamarine engagement ring Desi had given me. Within a few minutes our bedroom was swarming with police checking and taking fingerprints.

In the middle of all the excitement I excused myself and upchucked in the bathroom. "Don't be upset, Lucy darling," Desi comforted me. "I'll replace everything you lost."

I was sad about losing my jewelry—none of it was ever recovered—but that wasn't the half of it. I had been suffering from a nervous tummy in the morning for several weeks. That morning it occurred to me that I might be pregnant.

I was elated, nearly delirious, but I was also frightened. Now I was scared to do my act because it was so physically strenuous. In my seal act, I had to do a real belly whacker, flip over on my stomach three times, and slither offstage.

But I had six months' worth of contracts to fulfill. And I was so happy to be working with Desi again that I hated to call anything off until I was sure. I finished the week in Chicago and then we headed for the Roxy in New York. We arrived on a Friday and I immediately made arrangements for a pregnancy test, using my hairdresser's name at the laboratory to avoid publicity. Walter Winchell had once told me that he had spies in every big medical center in New York who provided him with inside tips about celebrities.

Sunday night Desi and I were in our dressing rooms at the Roxy, waiting for our next show. We alternated with a two-hour movie from morning until midnight, doing six or seven shows a day. Desi was fast asleep and I was knitting, listening to the radio. Walter Winchell came on the air and announced: "After ten childless years of marriage, Lucille Ball and Desi Arnaz are infanticipating." I dropped my knitting, ran into Desi's dressing room, and woke him up. "We're going to have a baby!"

Desi sat up, rubbing his eyes. "How d'ya know? We aren't supposed to hear until tomorrow!"

I said, "Winchell just told me."

"How d'ya like *∂at!*" was my Cuban's reaction.

Harriet, my hairdresser, Desi, and I did a jig of joy, shouting like Indians. I worked a few more weeks and then we canceled the rest of the bookings and flew home. Desi began adding a $23,000 nursery wing to our $17,000 house. It was two bedrooms and a shiny white tile room I called "the lab" with sterilizing, cooking, and laundry equipment. Desi even added an outside door at the far end of the playroom. "When our son's a teenager, he'll need a private entrance," he explained.

I sat idly in the garden at the ranch with wonderful, happy plans spinning through my mind. But in my third month, I miscarried. They kept me in the hospital for a week, doped with sedatives. I cried and cried, but the doctors assured me that I still had a chance to become a mother.

In the next three months I made the six-thousand-mile round trip to New York six weekends straight for television shows; I continued with my weekly radio show, *My Favorite Husband*, and had a painful kidney stone removed. And I kept urging my radio-television agent, Don Sharpe: *"Please find a way for Desi and me to do a television show together!"*

In October, Cecil B. DeMille offered me an exciting part in the circus spectacle he was casting, *The Greatest Show on Earth*. I had never worked with DeMille before and I accepted immediately.

My contract with Columbia called for one picture a year, but the late Harry Cohn, then head of that studio, hadn't come up with anything for me since *The Fuller Brush Girl*.

"Mr. Cohn," I asked him, "please let me out of my contract so I can do a picture at Paramount."

"What picture at Paramount?" he asked suspiciously.

"Mr. DeMille wants me for *Greatest Show on Earth*."

"Nothing doing." Mr. Cohn wouldn't let me out of my Columbia contract, nor would he let me do the DeMille movie, which meant so much to me. Harry Cohn was a hard-driving type and a ruthless fighter. He accomplished much and if you didn't expect the velvet glove treatment it was possible to get along with him. But this time, when he decided to get rough with me, I had had enough. I went right ahead with my costume fittings for DeMille's picture. I didn't know *how* I was going to outwit Harry Cohn in a legal way, but for once I was going to try.

A couple of weeks went by and Cohn sent me a script to read. It was a Sam Katzman production, or what is known in Hollywood as a lease breaker. Mr. Katzman's pictures were strictly class E. Anyone of any stature was supposed to say, "Over my dead body! I'll never do *that!*" and then Harry Cohn could cancel that player's contract without paying them off.

I had never feuded with a studio before and I wasn't about to earn the reputation of being difficult at this late date. I picked up the phone and called Harry Cohn. "I've just read the Sam Katzman script," I crooned into his ear. "I think it's *marvelous!* I'd be delighted to do it."

"You *would?*" Mr. Cohn almost fell over backward and poor Sam Katzman just about had a coronary. Mr. Cohn's plan had backfired. Under my contract I was to be paid $85,000 for my one remaining picture. My salary ate up half Katzman's budget. Harry was stuck with me; his ruse hadn't worked.

So I played an Arabian princess in Sam Katzman's *The Magic Carpet*—a temptress "whose lips and temper are hotter than the desert sands," as the promotion read. By the time I started *Magic Carpet*, five months after my miscarriage, I was pregnant again. It was fortunate that I wore voluminous belly dancer pants and cloaks, because I was getting fatter by the minute. It was important to keep this fact from Mr. Cohn, for then he could have canceled my contract immediately.

On the set, only Harriet knew my secret. Each night she let out the waist of my costume another notch or two. I collected eighty-five grand for a total of five days' work and got out of my Columbia contract very nicely. Then I went to see Mr. DeMille along with Desi.

With tears in my eyes, I told the great impresario,

"Mr. DeMille, I cannot do your picture, because I'm going to have a baby."

There was a long DeMille pause, a very dramatic pause. Mr. DeMille knew how much I loved the role and how important it was to me to appear in his picture. But he also knew I was almost forty years old; and he could hardly believe my news. Finally he turned to my husband and said, "Congratulations, Desi, you are the only person in the world to screw Harry Cohn, Columbia Pictures, Paramount, Cecil B. DeMille, and your wife, all at the same time."

His remark set all Hollywood laughing. Everybody, that is, except Harry Cohn. I had embarrassed him and cost him $85,000 along the way.

*The blissful mother- and
father-to-be at
the Desilu
Ranch.*

Chapter
11
♥

This time I decided that nothing was going to endanger my becoming a mother. I canceled everything except my radio show and sat placidly at home, knitting and waiting. The best year of my marriage to Desi was just before and after the birth of our first child. We exchanged no harsh words and experienced no upsets of any kind. Desi hovered about me, attentive to every need. I was grateful to God and in a complete daze of happiness.

Desi had a yellow convertible he usually drove at seventy and eighty miles an hour. As soon as he learned I was expecting again, he began driving as conservatively as an old lady.

He put up the convertible top and even rolled up all the windows to eliminate drafts and avoided every tiny bump in the road. The more conservative he became, the happier I grew. This was the way I'd always hoped our marriage would be.

When I was going into my fourth month of pregnancy, CBS suddenly gave Desi the green light: they would finance a pilot for a domestic television show featuring the two of us as a married couple. A show that might go on the air that fall.

"What show?" I asked our agent, Don Sharpe. "We don't have a television show."

"You've got a month to put one together," he answered. "They want the pilot by February fifteenth."

For ten years, Desi and I had been trying to become co-stars and parents; now our dearest goals were being realized much too fast. We suddenly felt unprepared for either and began to have second thoughts.

At that time, television was regarded as the enemy by Hollywood. So terrified was Hollywood of this medium, movie people were afraid to make even guest appearances. If I undertook a weekly television show and it flopped, I might never work in movies again.

It would mean each of us would have to give up our respective radio programs, and Desi would have to cancel all his band engagements. It was a tremendous gamble; it had to be an all-or-nothing commitment.

But this was the first real chance Desi and I would have to work together, something we'd both been longing for for years.

We continued to wrestle with the decision, trying to

look at things from every angle. Then one night Carole Lombard appeared to me in a dream. She was wearing one of those slinky bias-cut gowns of the thirties, waving a long black cigarette holder in her hand. "Go on, kid," she advised me airily. "Give it a whirl."

The next day I told Don Sharpe, "We'll do it. Desi and I want to work together more than anything else in the world."

We called my radio writers on *My Favorite Husband* and together dreamed up a set of television characters. Originally, we were Lucy and Larry López; it wasn't until we started our first shows that we became the Ricardos. Desi would be a Cuban bandleader who worked in New York City; I would play a housewife with burning stage ambitions.

Because we had so little time, we adapted parts of our vaudeville act for the pilot. I did a baggy-pants clown bit with the cello. For the rest of the show I appeared in bathrobe and pajamas to conceal my obvious condition. Desi sang, played the drums, and exchanged patter with me; he was the perfect partner, capable and funny, and his great charm and vitality came shining through.

A week later our agent phoned to say, "Philip Morris wants to sponsor you!" We were on our way.

However, in the next few weeks the deal twisted and changed and almost blew up. The sponsor had a second demand: they not only wanted a weekly show, they also wanted it done live in New York. In 1951, a show done live on the West Coast appeared on the East Coast in fuzzy kinescope — with the image about as sharp as a piece of cheesecloth.

We refused to move to New York. Desi suggested

that we *film* the show, live, in front of an audience. The network people screamed. A filmed show cost twice as much as a live one. The sponsor wouldn't put up more money and neither would CBS. So Desi made a canny offer: In return for a $1,000 weekly salary cut for us, we were given complete ownership of the show; originally, CBS had owned half of it. CBS also agreed to advance the enormous sums of money needed to start film production, with Desi as producer.

All Desi had ever managed was a sixteen-piece Latin band. Now he had to rent a studio and equipment and find actors, cameramen, stagehands, cutters, film editors, writers, and scripts for thirty-nine weekly shows.

When the deal was finally set, it was late March. We had to start filming by August 15 to be on the air by October. We could rehearse and film a half-hour show in a week, but cutting, editing, and scoring would take another five weeks at least.

We began discussing possible writers. First comes the script, and then the interpretation and improvisations. Both of us admired and liked my three radio writers, Madelyn Pugh, Bob Carroll, Jr., and Jess Oppenheimer. As Jess says, "In a show that's destined to be a hit, nothing but happy things happen. God's arm was around us."

As Lucy Ricardo, I played a character very much like Liz Cugat on my radio show. Lucy was impulsive, inquisitive, and completely feminine. She was never acid or vicious. Even with pie on her face she remained an attractive and desirable female, stirred by real emotions.

Lucy Ricardo's nutty predicaments arose from an

earnest desire to please. And there was something touching about her stage ambitions. As we were discussing her with our writers, Desi spoke up. "She tries so hard . . . she can't dance and she can't sing . . . she's earnest and pathetic. . . . Oh, I love that Lucy!" And so the title of the show was born.

Desi was cast as the steadying, levelheaded member of the family, a practical man and a good money manager. He tolerated his wife's foibles good-naturedly, but he could only be pushed so far. The audience had to believe that I lived in fear and trembling of my husband's wrath, and with Desi, they could. There was also a chemistry, a strong mutual attraction between us, which always came through.

At the very first story conference, Desi laid down the underlying principles of the show. The humor could never be mean or unkind. Neither Ricky nor Lucy would ever flirt seriously with anyone else. Mothers-in-law would not be held up to ridicule. Most of all, Desi insisted on Ricky's manhood. He refused to ever be a nincompoop husband. "When Lucy's got something up her sleeve that would make Ricky look like a fool, let the audience know that I'm in on the secret," he told our writers.

I had always known that Desi was a great showman, but many were surprised to learn he was a genius with keen instincts for comedy and plot. He has a quick, brilliant mind; he can instantly find the flaw in any story line; and he has inherent good taste and an intuitive knowledge of what will and will not play. He is a great producer, a great director. He never stays on too long or allows anybody else to.

When we had the characters of Lucy and Ricky clear

in our minds, Jess Oppenheimer suggested that we add another man and wife—an older couple in a lower income bracket. The writers could then pit couple against couple, and the men against the women. I had known Bill Frawley since my RKO starlet days as a great natural comic; we all agreed upon him for Fred Mertz. We then started thinking about a TV wife for Bill.

We considered a number of actresses, and then one day Desi heard about a fine actress from the Broadway stage named Vivian Vance. She was appearing that summer in *The Voice of the Turtle* at La Jolla Playhouse. The ride down the coast was too much for my advanced state of pregnancy, so Jess and Desi drove down without me. They liked how Vivian handled herself on the stage and the way she could flip a comedy line. So they hired her on the spot.

As far as I was concerned, it was Kismet. Viv and I were extraordinarily compatible. We both believe wholeheartedly in what we call "an enchanted sense of play," and use it liberally in our show. It's a happy frame of mind, the light touch, skipping into things instead of plodding. It's looking at things from a child's point of view and believing. The only way I can play a funny scene is to believe it. Then I can convincingly eat like a dog under a table, freeze to death beneath burning-hot klieg lights, or bake a loaf of bread ten feet long.

We had no way of knowing how comical she and Bill would be together. Vivian was actually much younger than Bill. Up until then, she'd usually been cast in glamorous "other woman" parts. But she went along gamely with Ethel Mertz's dowdy clothes, no false eyelashes or eye makeup, and hair that looked as if she had washed and set it herself. But she drew the line at padding her body to look fatter.

Time and again she told Jess Oppenheimer, "If my husband in this series makes fun of my weight and I'm actually fat, then the audience won't laugh . . . they'll feel sorry for me. But if he calls me a fat old bag and I'm not too heavy, then it will seem funny."

Vivian was unhappy in her marriage to actor Philip Ober and so she ate; after a while Jess stopped insisting that she pad herself. On summer vacations she'd diet, and once she came back on the set positively svelte. "Well, Vivian," I kidded her, "you've got just two weeks to get fat and sloppy again."

She and Bill scrapped a good deal, and this put a certain amount of real feeling into their stage quarrels. Bill became the hero of all henpecked husbands. He couldn't walk down the street without some man coming up to him and saying, "Boy, Fred, you tell that Ethel off something beautiful!"

So much good luck was involved in the casting. Early in the series, our writers wanted to write a show in which the Mertzes had to sing and dance. We then learned for the first time that both Vivian and Bill had had big musical comedy careers. Vivian had been in *Skylark* with Gertrude Lawrence, and Bill was a well-known vaudeville hoofer.

I had insisted upon having a studio audience; otherwise, I knew, we'd never hit the right tempo. We did the show every Thursday night in front of four hundred people, a cross-section of America. I could visualize our living and working together on the set like a stock company, then filming it like a movie, and at the same time staging it like a Broadway play. "We'll have opening night every week," I chortled.

Desi's first problem was that there were no movie studios in Hollywood with accommodations for an audience. We also wanted a stage large enough to film the show in its natural sequence, with no long delays setting up stage decorations or shifting lights.

Desi hired Academy Award–winning cameraman Karl Freund, whose work I had admired at MGM, and discussed the problems with him. Karl flew to New York for a week to see how television cameras could be moved around without interfering too much with the audience's view of the action. He came back pretty unimpressed. "There are no rules for our kind of show, so we'll make up our own."

Karl Freund hit upon a revolutionary new way of filming a show with three cameras shooting the action simultaneously. One of these cameras is far back, another recording the medium shots, with a third getting the close-ups. The film editor then has three different shots of a particular bit of action. By shifting back and forth between the three, he can get more variety and flexibility than with the one-camera technique.

But moving three huge cameras about the stage between the actors and the audience called for the most complex planning.

First Desi rented an unused movie studio. By tearing down partitions, he joined two giant soundstages. This gave us enough room to build three permanent sets—the Ricardo living room, bedroom, and kitchen—and a fourth set, which was sometimes the New York nightclub where Ricky worked and sometimes an alligator farm or a vineyard in Italy or the French Alps—whatever the script called for. We even turned that thirty-foot set into the deck of the USS *Constitution* once.

The roving cameras couldn't roll easily on the wooden stage, so a smooth concrete floor was laid down. Each week a complicated pattern of chalk instructions was drawn on the cement, indicating each camera's position for every shot. This is known as camera blocking, and took two full days.

Desi and I okayed each pillow, picture, pot, and pan that went into the Ricardos' apartment, to make sure it was authentically middle-income. While the three rooms slowly took form before our eyes, bleachers for three hundred people were built facing them. The Los Angeles Fire and Health departments threw a mountain of red tape at us when they learned we were inviting a large weekly audience into a movie studio. Desi had to add rest rooms, water fountains, and an expensive sprinkler system. Microphones were installed over the heads of the audience; we wanted our laughs live—some of the canned laughter you hear today came from our *Lucy* show audiences.

Desi and I were so excited and happy, planning our first big venture together. I thought that *I Love Lucy* was a pleasant little situation comedy that might even survive its first season. But my main thoughts centered on the baby. The nursery wing was now complete and I planned to have a natural delivery late in June. And so I happily waited, and waited, thirty pounds heavier than ever before. I was so proud of that big stomach of mine. Desi, knowing that my grandmother Flora Belle had been one of five sets of twins, expected triplets.

The weeks passed and still no baby. Finally my obstetrician decided on a cesarean delivery. Lucie Desirée Arnaz was lying sideways with her head just under my rib cage; when they performed the cesarean, the surgical knife missed her face by a hairsbreadth. But miss her it did; she was complete, healthy, and beautiful. She arrived at eight-fifteen a.m. on July 17, 1951, weighing seven pounds, eight ounces. Lyricist Eddie Maxwell wrote the words to a song in her honor, "There's a Brand-New Baby at Our House," and Desi sat up all night with his guitar composing the music. The next day, the proud papa passed out Havana cigars to his entire studio audience and introduced his new daughter and that song to the world on his new CBS radio show, *Tropical Trip*. Later on, it was used on the show when Lucy Ricardo had her baby.

The day that Lucie and I were to leave the hospital, Desi appeared in a long, dark blue sedan, our new "family" car. He drove us home at a sedate crawl and the baby and her nurse were installed in their private wing.

Lucie's coming changed our life completely. Before, there had been two professional people in the house, discussing deals and contracts and money matters and scripts. Now suddenly there was a fragile little new spark of life there, affecting everything we thought or did.

God . . . how I love babies! Not just my own, but the world's babies . . . I'm so sorry that I can't have any more. I had to go right back to work after Lucie was born, so I missed hours and hours and hours of her earliest life. When Lucie stopped sleeping most of the day, it got especially tough to leave her for the studio. Once there, I was seldom home again before midnight. During the early days of the *I Love Lucy* show, I only had Sundays free. So I spent this time entirely with my new baby, marveling at her.

It took me a long time to recover physically from Lucie's birth, but I had no time to pamper myself. Six weeks after she arrived, I walked on the *Lucy* set to start filming the series.

Rehearsals got under way to the pounding of hammers and buzzing of saws; the set was only half built and a whole wall of the soundstage was still missing when we started. Desi was so nervous that he memorized everybody's lines and moved his own lips as they spoke; he also kept flicking his eyes around the stage watching the progress of the three cameras. He soon got over this, but proved to be the fastest learner of dialogue.

To my delight, I discovered that the *I Love Lucy* show drew from everything I'd learned in the movies, radio, the theater, and vaudeville. I wanted everything about the venture to be top-flight: the timing, the handling of props, the dialogue. We argued a good deal at first because we all cared so passionately; sometimes we'd discuss phrasing or word emphasis in a line of dialogue until past midnight. Bill Frawley couldn't understand the need for all this hairsplitting. He'd tear his part out of the script, memorize it, and pay no attention to what the rest of us were saying or doing. Vivian, like me, was a perfectionist who took her profession very seriously. "Now what's my motivation here?" she'd ask me or Desi or Jess, and this would launch a half-hour discussion. Bill couldn't have cared less. If he got his big laugh, he didn't care how or why. And actually, Bill can be funny doing nothing. He has that kind of face, and in any kind of costume he's hilarious.

During one early rehearsal, Vivian was championing a particular way in which a line should be spoken. Nobody agreed with her, but she kept explaining and explaining, until finally we did see the logic of her position. By this time it was two a.m. and she was so wound up she couldn't stop talking. She went on and on until Desi tapped her gently on the shoulder. "Vivian, your yo-yo string is tangled."

I could sense a flaw in the story line or dialogue but I couldn't always put my objections into words. Frustrated, Desi would burst into a flood of Spanish. I'd express my frustrations by getting mad. Vivian was a tower of strength in such circumstances; she would intuitively guess what was wrong and then analyze it. She would make a great director.

We rehearsed the first show twelve hours a day. Then on Friday evening, August 15, 1951, the bleachers filled up by eight o'clock and Desi explained to the audience that they would be seeing a brand-new kind of television show. He stepped behind the curtain and we all took our places.

Sitting in the bleachers that first night were a lot of anxious rooters: DeDe and Desi's mother, Dolores; our writers; Andrew Hickox; and a raft of Philip Morris representatives and CBS officials. To launch the series, the network had paid out $300,000. They hoped it would last long enough to pay back that advance.

We were lucky all the way. The first four shows put us among the top ten on television. Arthur Godfrey, one of the giants, preceded us and urged his watchers to stay tuned to *I Love Lucy*. Our twentieth show made us number one on the air and there we stayed for three wild, incredible years.

I Love Lucy has been called the most popular television show of all time. Such national devotion to one show can never happen again; there are too many shows, on many more channels, now. But in 1951–1952, our show changed the Monday-night habits of America. Between nine and nine-thirty, taxis disappeared from the streets of New York. Marshall Fields department store in Chicago hung up a sign: "We Love Lucy too, so from now on we will be open Thursday nights instead of Monday." Telephone calls across the nation dropped sharply during that half hour, as well as the water flush rate, as whole families sat glued to their seats.

That season Red Skelton got the Emmy Award in February 1952, but told the nation, "You gave this to the wrong redhead. I don't deserve this. It should go to Lucille Ball." During our first season someone told Desi that our show had a hit rating of 70. He looked worried, thinking that a "grade" of 70 was barely passing. "You're kidding," he said, not realizing that a rating of 70 was indeed phenomenal.

♥

In May 1952, Desi and I both walked into Jess Oppenheimer's office, elated.

"Well, amigo," Desi told Jess, "we've just heard from the doctor. Lucy's having another baby in January. So we'll have to cancel everything. That's the end of the show."

My feelings were mixed. I felt bad for the cast, the crew, and the writers. I regretted that our dream of working together was again busted. But my predominant feeling was still one of elation. Another baby! And I was almost forty-one!

Jess sat looking at us silently. Then he remarked casually, "I wouldn't suggest this to any other actress in the world—but why don't we continue the show and have a baby on TV?"

Desi's face lit up. "Do you think we could? Would it be in good taste?" No actress had ever appeared in a stage or television play before when she was obviously pregnant.

"We'll call the CBS censor and see," said Jess. That wonderful guy said, "I don't see why not," and with his active encouragement, Philip Morris and the network went along with it. We had just finished forty *Lucy* shows, ten months of backbreaking work with hardly a letup, but now we made feverish plans to get into production for the next season as fast as possible.

The baby would be delivered by cesarean section, so we had a definite date to plan around: January 19. We took only a two-week vacation that summer, beginning the new shows in June. All through the hot, steaming Hollywood summer we worked, ten and twelve hours a day, six days a week.

In the early fall, when I was beginning to look pretty big, we did seven shows concerning my pregnancy. These films were screened by a priest, a minister, and a rabbi for any possible violation of good taste. It was the CBS network that objected to using the word "pregnant." They made us say "expecting." The three-man religious committee protested, "What's wrong with 'pregnant'?" They were heartily in favor of what we were doing: showing motherhood as a happy, wholesome, normal family event.

Many times on the *Lucy* show the script was very close to reality. In real life Desi and I had separated and reconciled many times, and the public knew this. So our writers did a script about Lucy and Ricky quarreling and separating. Ricky Ricardo moved out of the apartment and I was supposed to walk around the living room set, forlorn, touching each piece of furniture wistfully.

To our writers' amazement, people in the studio audience took out their handkerchiefs and started weeping. Then when Ricky and Lucy were reconciled a few minutes later, in what was supposed to be a hilarious scene, nobody laughed. They were too happy and relieved to see us together again.

Because the audience knew that Desi and I were really married, they assumed that Vivian Vance and Bill Frawley were, too. When Desi would announce, "And here's Vivian's *real* husband, Philip Ober!" they would sit in stunned disbelief. Even Vivian's father was caught up in the make-believe. "Why don't you use your own name on the show?" he asked Vivian. "Fred Mertz does."

Both times I was pregnant, I mooned for hours over a baby photograph of Desi, hoping by some magic I would have a baby who looked just like him. Then we did a show where Lucy tells Ricky she is having a baby. She sends an anonymous note to him at his nightclub, requesting that he sing "Rock-a-Bye Baby." Ricky complies, going from table to table singing the old nursery rhyme. In front of Lucy's table, he looks into her eyes and suddenly realizes that *he* is the father. When we did this scene before an audience, Desi was suddenly struck by all the emotion he'd felt when we discovered, after ten childless years of marriage, that we were finally going to have Lucie. His eyes filled up and he couldn't finish the song; I started to cry, too. Vivian started to sniffle; even the hardened stagehands wiped their eyes with the backs of their hands. The director wanted retakes at the end of the show, but the audience stood up and shouted, "No, no!"

Lucille and Lucie inspect Desi, Jr., on his christening day, 1953.

Chapter 12

♥

The birth of little Desi has been described in a college history textbook as one of the great emotional events of 1953. I had quit doing the shows in November, when I was carrying thirty-three extra pounds. During the following seven weeks, we aired the sequence involving my pregnancy (filmed in September and October but shown on TV screens in December and January).

The baby's birth had been scheduled for Monday morning, January 19, at the Cedars of Lebanon Hospital. We had tried to keep the date a secret, but the news had leaked out that my real baby and Lucy Ricardo's fake baby would arrive on the same day. Flowers and telegrams in great profusion preceded my trip to the hospital. When Desi took me in that Sunday night, the bouquets already filled my room and half the corridor. One wire from a good friend read, "Well, don't just lie there—do something."

They doped me up with pills, but I lay awake all night anyway. I had the same feelings of terror and desperate hope that any mother has. "Oh God," I prayed, "just make it a normal, healthy baby." During the early-morning operation I was conscious the whole time. At 8:20 a.m., my baby was born—Desiderio Alberto Arnaz IV. At last Desi had a son and heir to carry on his proud family traditions.

That afternoon I awoke to find Desi sitting on my bed sobbing. There were seven thousand letters and a thousand telegrams waiting for me. But this was only the beginning. Counting the telegrams, letters, cards, phone calls, baby bootees, and other gifts, one million people sent some expression of their good wishes for the new baby.

Desi went to the Brown Derby that day, threw his hands up to the ceiling, and shouted, "Now we got everythin'."

The national hysteria continued for weeks. The same day our little Desi was born, forty-four million Americans watched the arrival of Ricky Ricardo, Jr., on the *I Love Lucy* show. The next day, Eisenhower was inaugurated as President, and the following Sunday night Walter Winchell said on the air, "This was a banner week: the nation got a man and Lucy got a boy."

This was a banner year in all respects for Desi and me.

In February, we won two Emmy Awards—Best Comic Actress and Best Comedy Show—and Desi clinched an $8 million deal with Philip Morris, making us television's highest-paid stars. In March, two months after little Desi's birth, I went back to work. In June, we were named Husband and Wife of the Year. We took three days off from the show and then went directly into production of MGM's *The Long, Long Trailer.*

We did this movie for my old friend producer Pandro Berman. My former studio, MGM, paid us $250,000, and fortunately the show was a big moneymaker. I had Lana Turner's old dressing room and Desi was in Clark Gable's. We took one month's vacation, then went right back to Stage 9 again for the *Lucy* show. During all this period I was not getting my rest. I felt terribly tired.

The smash success of our TV show and the physical strain of combining my last pregnancy with a full work schedule took its toll. I developed a feeling I couldn't shake. All our good fortune was suddenly going to vanish. When I tore myself away from my babies in the morning, I had this terrible fear that they'd be gone when I returned at night. Having the love and adoration of millions was wonderful and thrilling, but I could have done with half of our *Lucy* success, for with it came a lot of new stress.

Desi had managed to cut our shooting schedule down to five days a week, but evenings and Saturdays and Sundays our house was filled with people running in and out consulting Desi on deals. By this time he was producing other shows and giving technical assistance to still others. We had signed a ten-year lease on the Motion Picture Center in Hollywood, which we eventually bought for $750,000, and Desi was deeply involved in the reconstruction of four soundstages and hundreds of offices. He estimated correctly that by the end of 1953, Desilu would have completed ninety hours of film production and would be doing a gross business of millions of dollars.

In addition to the production company, we also had a merchandising business. It was possible to furnish a house and dress a whole family with items carrying our *I Love Lucy* label. Red Skelton did a hilarious TV skit poking fun at this. As he walked into his house, his wife shouted, "Don't track mud on my *I Love Lucy* rug!" As he started to sink into a chair, she added, "Don't mess up my *I Love Lucy* chair!" He finally shoots her, and she moans, "You shot a bullet through my *I Love Lucy* blouse!"

One baby food company offered us $50,000 to use little Desi's name on their product, but we wouldn't even consider that, even though it was the same baby food he ate.

In the middle of August 1953, we settled into a rented house on the beach in Del Mar, California, with both babies, a nurse, Desi's mother, and an assortment of houseguests. It was then that I received a call that seemed to realize my anxious apprehension. The call was from William A. Wheeler, an investigator for the House Un-American Activities Committee. The committee wanted to hold a closed hearing with me, DeDe, and Freddy on September 4, in Hollywood.

With good friend Dick Powell in
Meet the People. *Lucille always*
admired Dick for his levelheadedness
and his ability to maintain a sane
and loving family life in
show business.

Lucille and Van Johnson rhumba to Desi's Latin rhythms, as Desi and his orchestra break attendance records at Ciro's in Hollywood, circa 1947. Since Van was also in the film Too Many Girls, *where Lucille and Desi met, he always kidded them by saying, "It could've been me, Lucy!"*

Under Desi's expert tutelage Lucille learned to enjoy fishing from their boat.

Lucille and Desi with their proud mothers, Dolores and DeDe, celebrate the couple's second wedding ceremony at Chatsworth, June 19, 1949.

*Lucille, with her favorite leading man,
Bob Hope, in a scene from* Fancy Pants,
also starring Lee Bowman, 1950.

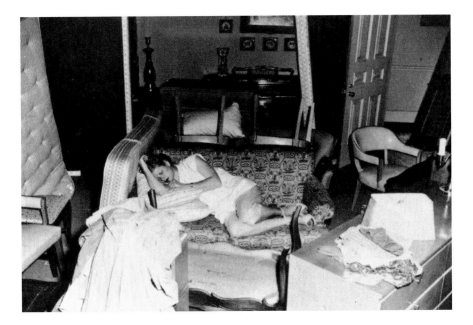

*Free for a few minutes, the expectant mother catnaps
on a couch on the* I Love Lucy *set.*

*Celebrating Lucie Desiree's first birthday, at
Chatsworth, July 17, 1952.*

The Arnaz family on the cover of LOOK *magazine, April 1953.*

On September 12, 1953, the press announces that Lucille has been completely cleared of all communist affiliation.

Lucille and Lucie share a cribside laugh with Desi, Jr., 1953.

Lucille and Desi with director Vincente Minnelli and his daughter, Liza, on the set of The Long, Long Trailer, *1954.*

A family stroll in front of their new house in Palm Springs.

Lucille and Desi seem pleased with the progress of their new house in Palm Springs, and pleased with each other as well.

Much of I Love Lucy's *success is widely credited to Desi's directorial skills and his keen instinct for comedy. Here, he makes the audience laugh, and puts to rest their fears of being unable to see all the action with the three moving cameras in front of them.*

The "Ricardos" and the "Mertzes" of I Love Lucy.

Lucille and Desi welcome hundreds of Desilu employees and their families to their annual company picnic, 1955.

Lucille and Desi thank the viewing public for making them number one in the ratings, yet again. November 1957.

NIELSEN TOTAL AUDIENCE	
First Report for November, 1957	
1. Lucille Ball-Desi Arnaz	57.5
2. Gunsmoke	44.1
3. Ed Sullivan Show	41.6
4. Perry Como Show	40.9
5. Tales of Wells Fargo	38.6
6. Danny Thomas Show	37.6
7. Jack Benny Show	37.2
8. Cheyenne	37.2
9. Wyatt Earp	36.3
10. Jerry Lewis Show	36.1

NIELSEN AVERAGE AUDIENCE	
First Report for November, 1957	
1. Lucille Ball-Desi Arnaz	47.0
2. Gunsmoke	42.0
3. Tales of Wells Fargo	36.0
4. Danny Thomas Show	35.5
5. Jack Benny Show	34.3
6. Wyatt Earp	34.2
7. Ed Sullivan Show	32.2
8. Perry Como Show	32.0
9. I've Got A Secret	31.9
10. Have Gun, Will Travel	31.6

THANKS

TRENDEX	
November, 1957	
1. Lucille Ball-Desi Arnaz	40.2
2. Jerry Lewis	34.3
3. Perry Como	32.7
4. Gunsmoke	32.3
5. Wyatt Earp	29.2
6. Wells Fargo	28.9
7. Jack Benny	28.6
8. Person to Person	27.9
9. Danny Thomas	27.3
10. What's My Line	27.2
Reprinted from Variety	

ARB	
November, 1957	
1. LUCY & DESI	44.6
2. Gunsmoke	42.5
3. Perry Como	42.5
4. Tales of Wells Fargo	35.5
5. Restless Gun	33.3
6. People Are Funny	33.1
7. G.E. Theatre	32.7
8. Lassie	32.7
9. Twenty-One	32.6
10. Ernie Ford	32.4
10. What's My Line?	32.4
Reprinted from Variety	

Desilu

Jamestown welcomes hometown girl, Lucille, and her husband, Desi, during their national tour to promote their 1956 movie, Forever Darling.

Lucille and Desi with longtime friend actress June Havoc.

I Love Lucy revealed Desi's multiple talents—producer, director, actor, musician, and inventor of the three-camera method for filming television, which revolutionized the industry. (Photo by Leonard Nadel.)

Lucille and Lucie, Vivian and Desi, Jr., on a sleigh ride when The Lucy-Desi Comedy Hour *was filmed at Sun Valley, Idaho, April 1958.*

During their hiatus from the I Love Lucy *show, Lucille, Desi, and the children often escaped to Hawaii.*

The two Desis in a conga-drum duet at their summer home in Del Mar, California, in 1958.

Lucille's burro takes the lead as Lucie and Desi, Jr., follow on the cobblestone streets of Capri, 1959.

Lucille starring on Broadway in Wildcat, *1961.*

Lucille in her Lexington Avenue apartment in New York, where she and the children lived during the Broadway run of Wildcat *(1960–61).*

Lucille with friend Bob Hope and ex-husband Desi Arnaz, sharing a laugh, 1961.

Lucille in front of the family home at 1000 North Roxbury Drive in Beverly Hills.

Freddy, now a salesman in Phoenix, Arizona, joined us at Del Mar and we drove up together. Investigator Wheeler went over some statements we had made the previous year to the FBI about my "Communist connections."

What had happened was that when Dore Schary and Larry Parks were subpoenaed to go to Washington in the late 1940s to appear before the House Un-American Activities Committee, Bill Holden and I went on the air to support them. We did that at the request of the Screen Writers Guild; when my own union told me my support was needed, I didn't ask questions. Then after I spoke my piece for Schary and Parks, some scandal-sheet reporter went through all the voting records to see how I had registered over the years, and he found that in 1936 I registered as a Communist.

That was the year my grandfather Fred held all his political meetings in our garage at 1344 North Ogden Drive. He had a friend running for city council on the Communist ticket and he insisted that DeDe, Freddy, and I register so we could vote for him.

We did it to please Daddy. He'd had one stroke already and the least little argument got him all upset.

So in the spring of 1952 I talked to some FBI men for several hours at a meeting arranged at the ranch. The records showed that I had registered as a Communist voter in 1936. I never voted, however, and after two years, my registration lapsed. The FBI said that I had once been named to the California State Central Committee of the Communist Party. I said this was news to me and that if my name was there, it was listed without my knowledge or consent. They also said that a member of the Communist party had testified that she attended meetings at 1344 North Ogden Drive during 1936 and had never seen me at any of these meetings.

I told the investigators that during 1936 I had been working at the RKO studios and in Lela Rogers's Little Theater group, six and seven days a week. I was seldom home before midnight and then I was only interested in getting some sleep, not attending a political meeting.

The FBI men seemed satisfied. As far as they were concerned, I was cleared. They called me "politically immature" and saw no reason for further investigation of what was essentially an impulsive, emotional step I'd taken in my youth for the sake of my grandfather.

So I had put the whole business out of my mind, until I got Wheeler's call in Del Mar, in August of the following year.

At the hearing held September 4, 1953, in Hollywood, I told him about my registering as a Communist in 1936, "I was of a mind to try and do something that would please Daddy. It just didn't seem like such an awful thing to do, the way it does these days . . . it was almost as terrible to be a Republican then."

Then I was asked about a petition I had read over the radio about the plight of the Okies. I explained that a studio official had asked me to read it and that I had been excused from a picture to do so.

According to my testimony, which was officially recorded that day, I swore: "I have never done anything for the Communists, to my knowledge, at any time. I have never contributed money or attended a meeting or had anything to do with people connected with it, if to my knowledge they were. I am not a Communist now. I have never been. I never wanted to be. Nothing in the world could ever change my mind. At no time in my life have I ever been in sympathy with anything that even faintly resembled it."

Again we were completely cleared and assured that none of the secret testimony would go beyond the walls of that hearing room.

But two days later, on Sunday night, September 6, 1953, I was home alone at the ranch in Chatsworth with our two children, listening to Walter Winchell's radio program, when he came out with a blind item: "What top redheaded television comedienne has been confronted with her membership in the Communist party?" (I remember thinking, "Oh my gosh, do they think Imogene Coca is a Communist?") When Desi called from our beach house in Del Mar, where he'd spent the weekend with some poker buddies, he said, "Lucy, were you listening to Winchell tonight?"

"Of course, you know I always do. Do you believe that about Imogene?"

"Lucy," he said, as if scolding a small child, "he's not talking about Coca! He means you!"

"Me?" I said, as my knitting went flying. "How can he?"

"I'm on my way home—we'll be expecting some people about one a.m.," he told me.

"Why? What are you having, a party?"

"No, honey," he said seriously. "You're in trouble."

For years I had known about Hollywood's insidious "blacklist." The mere accusation of Red activity against someone—a writer, actor, or director—could put that person under a permanent cloud whether he was guilty or not. An actor could be "cleared" for one show and not for another—all on the same network. A writer could be denied credit for his work or find himself permanently unemployed by any studio. Television sponsors, fearing a boycott of their goods, quaked in their boots if anyone on their shows was even remotely tinged with the label of "controversial."

The most vicious thing about this blacklist was that anyone—even the most ignorant crank—could point the finger at someone and the charge could hold.

I had now gone through two closed-door hearings on the matter—before the FBI and the Un-American Activities Committee—and been cleared by both. But Walter Winchell's broadcast could still ruin me. I don't blame Walter Winchell. He had heard that the charge against me was going to be publicized in a magazine. He wanted a scoop; that's what he's paid for. But he might at least have been accurate.

That Sunday night, Desi quickly rounded up Desilu officials, including our public relations man, Kenneth Morgan, who was then married to my cousin Cleo, along with press relations men from MGM, CBS, and Philip Morris. Our movie for MGM, *The Long, Long Trailer,* was not yet released, so the studio was also interested in protecting its investment in me.

I told them all about my voting registration back in

1936. When they learned that I had been cleared by both the FBI and the congressional committee, they decided that nothing further need be done. Perhaps it would all blow over.

Two days passed. Then on Wednesday, September 9, Winchell's nationally syndicated column repeated the same statement he had made on the air. On Thursday, Jack O'Brien of the *New York Journal-American* wrote, "Lucille Ball plans to retire in four years. She will retire a lot sooner than she thinks."

On Friday, the hot news broke. This was the day we'd planned to film the first show of the fall season. I rose early, as usual. Through the window I saw two strange men in hats standing near our orchard. I woke Desi up. Still in his pajamas, he opened the door and asked what the men wanted. They said they were police reporters from the *Los Angeles Herald-Express,* sent to talk to me about my "Communist activities."

Desi said firmly that I had no statement to make. We dressed as fast as we could and slipped out the back door. At the Desilu studios, twenty-five miles away, everything was pandemonium. Reporters were everywhere; a cacophony of phones rang. By noon, the *Herald-Express* had a three-inch headline: "Lucille Ball Named Red." Two hours later, New Yorkers read in their five o'clock evening papers, "America's Most Beloved Comedienne is Communist."

It seemed to Desi and me that the first statement to the press should come from the Un-American Activities Committee, so I kept mum and away from reporters. In the morning I sat under the hair dryer in pin curls, as usual, and did my nails. My hands shook. In the afternoon I went through hours of comedy rehearsal, white-faced and with a devastating headache.

Alfred Lyons, board chairman of Philip Morris, phoned me and said, "Lucy, I want to ask you one yes-or-no question: Are you a Communist?"

"No," I said.

"That's good enough for me," he said. "If you want, you can cancel the show we planned for tonight. Take the full half hour of our TV time and explain to the public in any way you like what this nonsense is all about."

I burst into tears and thanked him. I would have spoken to America, except that at six o'clock that evening Representative Donald L. Jackson, chairman of the House Un-American Activities Committee, called a press conference in his Hollywood hotel room and cleared me completely.

Jackson, a California Republican, had spent the day phoning the majority of the other committee members, and his statement was authorized by them. He told reporters that I had freely admitted having registered as a Communist in 1936, but that there was no evidence that I had ever belonged to the Communist party, or voted Communist, or attended any Communist meeting, or even known that my name had been listed on the party's state committee.

He said that the House committee had known about my registration for a year and had not thought it fair to divulge it, but that "independent investigators" had come across the record recently. The consequent spreading of rumors had threatened "irreparable damage" to Miss Ball.

Desi brought me the news of Representative Jackson's statement in my dressing room. "Today I've learned who my friends are," I told him. This official clearance meant that we could go on with the show. But before me was the terrible ordeal of facing an audience packed with reporters and curiosity-seekers. I stood waiting for my cue with a face white as chalk. A doctor stood by because, as Vivian said later, "I think if Lucy had heard one boo from that audience, she'd have collapsed."

Desi gave the warm-up in his usual breezy way. "Welcome to the first *I Love Lucy* show of the season," he said. "We are glad to have you back, and we're glad to be back ourselves. But before we go on, I want to talk to you about something serious. Something very serious. You all know what it is. The papers have been full of it all day."

He had a little typed speech in his hand but at this point he tucked it into his pocket. His voice broke and then he went on with deep emotion. "Lucy has never been a Communist—not now—and never will be." The audience applauded for a full minute. "I was kicked out of Cuba," Desi continued, "because of Communism. We despise everything about it. Lucy is as American as Bernie Baruch and Ike Eisenhower. . . . On Saturday the complete transcript of Lucy's testimony will be released to the papers and you can read it for yourself."

The audience stood up and cheered. Someone yelled, "We're with you, boy." Desi then introduced Bill Frawley and Vivian Vance, who came out and smiled. Then he said, "Now I want you to meet my favorite wife, my favorite redhead—in fact, that's the only thing *red* about her, and even that's not legitimate—Lucille Ball."

Feeling as stiff as an iron poker, I walked out into the limelight. I couldn't speak, but my features were fraught with emotion. Still speechless, with tears in my eyes, I turned and walked back through the curtains.

My years of rigid self-discipline paid off that night. I lost myself in *Lucy* and clowned and cavorted without a sign of strain. At the end of the show, the cast came out as usual for a farewell bow. My Lucy voice—that high, bubbly, childlike voice—dropped to my normal low tones. "God bless you for being so kind," I told them. Finally, in my dressing room, I gave way to the tears I had been holding in since early morning.

True to Desi's promise, we had fifty copies or more made of my testimony before William Wheeler and distributed them to the press at the ranch the next afternoon. Among the thirty reporters there to receive them were many who had known me since my Goldwyn Girl days; I considered them firm friends. Still, I was understandably nervous as Desi distributed the sheets of testimony I had given under oath. The reporters sat soberly reading for ten minutes or so. Then one of them stood up and said to his colleagues, "I think we owe both Desi and Lucy a vote of thanks for this chance to set the record straight, and I think a lot of irresponsible people owe them an apology."

Someone asked me how Walter Winchell found out about my registration.

"Walter Winchell," I replied, "knew I was *pregnant* before I did."

Desi told them, "William Wheeler told Lucy after he heard her testimony that she was politically immature. Hell, she couldn't even tell you who the governor of California was last year. And her grandfather was a character right out of *You Can't Take It With You.*"

Winchell apologized for his inaccurate reporting the following night—just one week after his words had initiated the furor. If our sponsor had canceled our contract, it was entirely likely that no sponsor or network would have been willing to carry us; and with the fall of the *Lucy* show, Desilu Productions would have collapsed too, affecting thousands of people and costing us millions of dollars.

As it was, only one store in the whole country canceled orders for *I Love Lucy* merchandise. I received over four thousand letters, of which only two were critical. In the following months, I was chosen Television's Woman of the Year for the second time, and President Eisenhower invited me and Desi to dinner at the White House. And *Lucy* remained the number-one show in popularity in the United States.

I was one of the lucky ones. For a long time, people in Hollywood couldn't get a job because of unfounded and vicious smear rumors. If news of my registration had been revealed during the worst witch-hunting days—between 1945 and 1950—my career probably would have been finished.

Jack Gould later wrote about this incident in the *New York Times:* "For once the accusation and rebuttal became known simultaneously and the public had an opportunity to judge and act for itself. Did millions of viewers as one man swear to forgo Philip Morris cigarettes because seventeen years ago Miss Ball registered as a Communist voter? To the contrary, they deluged her with wires of support."

He added, "The courteous and fair treatment which she was accorded should not be unique but rather should become standard for cases of this kind. . . . Broadcasting should study Miss Ball's case to see whether . . . it does not provide a formula for handling its loyalty problem with far more maturity and equity than previously have been displayed. The procedure that is available to the biggest star should also be available to the bit player in similar trouble."

♥

When *I Love Lucy* was in the middle of its third season, Desi and I decided to take a break and fly to New York for a few days' rest. We knew that we were number one on TV, and we'd just been told that nobody went to the john during the half hour we were on Monday nights. But we hadn't begun to realize the tremendous impact of television. We commuted between the ranch and the studio from Monday to Friday, and on weekends saw other show business people, just as we had in the old days. In Hollywood, you generally work and party with your colleagues. It makes for an isolated sort of life. As Frank Capra once said, "In Hollywood, we learn about life from each other's pictures."

We knew that MGM had a few things lined up for us

to promote *The Long, Long Trailer,* which was having its New York premiere, but mainly our idea was to have a short vacation from the daily grind. The trip started one Wednesday night in February 1954, with a tearful good-bye at the ranch to Lucie, age two and a half, and Desi, who was one. It was the first time we'd left them for more than a day or two.

We flew through the night toward New York so fast that I never had time to get my girdle off. We sat up all night. The plane's water pipes froze, making it impossible to freshen up before getting off. We landed at Idlewild at seven a.m. and were flabbergasted to be met by a huge crowd, a host of dignitaries, and a sixteen-piece German marching band. Desi and I mugged and hugged, then kissed and waved before sashaying down a red carpet stretching from the plane to the terminal.

When you're a movie star, your public image can still be vague because you look a little bit different in each picture. When you're seen in public, people nudge each other and whisper, "Is that . . . ?" and generally come up with the wrong name. But we soon discovered that when you play a continuing character on television, even if they've only seen you on the screen once or twice, everyone on the street recognizes you instantly.

Desi and I were bowled over by the number of people who stopped us on the streets in New York and the nice things they said. One afternoon we went down to the Seventh Avenue garment district to talk to the manufacturer of *I Love Lucy* dresses. It tickled me when a tousle-haired old woman threw open the window of her tenement apartment and called admiringly to us, "Say, Lucy, that guy of yours sure gives you hell!"

Our first night in New York we made a personal appearance on the stage of Radio City Music Hall, the first time the management had ever allowed such a promotion for a picture. "We've had many wonderful thrills in our life, Lucy and I," Desi told the audience, "but when we were sitting at home and got the phone call telling us that our first movie together was going to open at Radio City Music Hall . . . and that we were going to play the most famous theater in the world . . . together . . . we knew it was one of the greatest thrills we could ever have."

I wore a beautiful white chiffon gown with all my diamonds; Desi was in black tie. "I've always dreamed of walking across the stage of the Music Hall," I told the audience, and did just that, from one end to the other.

Back in our dressing rooms after our appearance, I felt an immense weariness. We'd been on the go for forty-eight hours, with only a brief hour's catnap on the plane. But Desi wouldn't hear of heading for bed. "Miss the chance to see our opening at the Music Hall? Are you crazy?" No promise of seeing the movie some other day would deter him, so we all headed for the loges.

Milton Berle, a close friend, came to pay his respects after the picture. "You know that scene where the trailer almost went off the cliff?" he asked us. "Ten more feet and *I'd* have been number one!"

The night following our Music Hall appearance, Desi and I went to see *Kind Sir,* with Mary Martin and Charles Boyer. We arrived late at the theater, just as the first curtain was going up, and scurried to our seats as unobtrusively as possible. During the first intermission, Mary Martin sent us a note to please come to her dressing room; after a pleasant chat we returned to our seats while the houselights were still up.

We sat there talking until we noticed a little hubbub of voices and the buzz-buzz of excited recognition. "Mrs. Roosevelt must be here," I told Desi.

We craned our necks toward the back of the theater and then we heard applause and saw people getting up. So we stood up too, clapping and looking around for the former First Lady. Then we realized the ovation was for us!

Every time we tried to sit down, the applause grew louder. They had to hold the curtain. This was the shocker of all time, as far as Desi and I were concerned.

The next night we had dinner with the Charles Ruggleses and then hurried late to the theater to see *Teahouse of the August Moon.* When the lights went up after the first act, there was a murmur of voices which grew into shouts and cheers. What with people hanging over the balcony yelling, "Hey, Ricky!" and, "Lucy, we love you!" and requesting autographs, they had to hold the second curtain a good long time. Then they brought the lights down dim and Davy Wayne, God bless him, came out in Japanese kimono and bowed and said, "We too rove Rucy."

The following night we had a dinner-and-theater date

with June Havoc and her husband, Bill Spier. As we ate a quiet dinner in our hotel suite, Desi and I told them about our lampooning at the Circus Saints and Sinners luncheon at the Waldorf, and about the spontaneous ovations which had greeted us everywhere: at blasé "21," at the Copacabana, and at every theater. June listened politely, if a bit wide-eyed, and said, "Well, I'm certainly looking forward to going to the theater with you two tonight. This is going to be pretty interesting."

Now of course, the minute she said that, I started thinking, "Oh God, what if it *doesn't* happen tonight?" I mean, Desi and I had been bouncing around town for three days and the excitement was bound to die down. Desperate not to be embarrassed and humiliated, I started trying to analyze why and how we had gotten all those standing ovations, and decided it was because no one saw us until intermission, and all recognized us at the same time, which must have helped create all the extra excitement. So now I'm doing anything I can think of to delay our arrival until the lights are down. I'm pretending I can't find my gloves, dropped an earring . . . Nothing works. We arrive a few minutes before curtain. The four of us walk through the lobby and down to our orchestra seats. Nothing.

I'm desperate now. I can't believe I did this, but I turned all the way around and nonchalantly looked up toward the balcony—the couple behind us smiled. I was afraid to even *look* at Havoc. When I sat down in my seat, she was still standing, just staring deadpan at me. Seconds later we were in *tears,* we laughed so hard. She'll never let me forget it!

You have to learn to live with recognition and fame,

and more important, you have to realize *why* you're famous. The *I Love Lucy* show was love personified. It was little domestic spats and upsets happily concluded, an exaggeration of American life that came out all right.

The next morning we learned that *The Long, Long Trailer* was definitely a hit. The Radio City Music Hall had enjoyed the biggest Sunday and Washington's Birthday in its entire history, with lines stretching from the theater clear to Fifth Avenue. Metro booked an additional $1.5 million of showings across the country following this news. I was particularly pleased to be able to be a moneymaker for Pandro Berman, the producer of the picture and my old boss at RKO. He must have been thinking to himself, "My God! She finally made it in pictures!"

I did a lot of thinking during our warm and tumultuous New York welcome. "For ten hot minutes you're such a great celebrity," I told myself. "Ten minutes later you're just another actress." Hedda Hopper says that I am one of the few actresses in Hollywood who survived my encounter with success in a single piece, only slightly battered as a consequence. There are many days when I feel more than slightly battered.

For there's a lot of masochism in the acting profession. We're willing to take a lot of punishment, but the minute we hit a little bit of success we are liable to run from it. We're frightened of it and develop all kinds of phobias as a consequence. Outsiders who don't understand think we have a chip on our shoulder, but it's not that at all. We're so used to failure, to being hurt and rebuffed, that we can easily come unhinged by success.

Vivian, Desi, and Lucille celebrate
I Love Lucy's Emmy Award
for Best Situation Comedy,
February 11, 1954.
Vivian also won that year for
Best Supporting Actress.

Chapter 13

♥

While we were at the peak of our popularity with *I Love Lucy*, I continued to feel guilt-ridden and anxious. "I don't deserve all this love and adulation," I said to myself. I couldn't believe my two beautiful, healthy babies were really mine; I kept half expecting some terrible tragedy to happen to them.

I'll always be grateful to Mrs. Charles Ruggles for taking me to hear Dr. Norman Vincent Peale for the first time during our big New York welcome. Listening to the doctor speak in his Marble Collegiate Church, I was moved to tears. Here was a man who spoke my language, who offered me a practical, everyday kind of religion. We have kept in close touch ever since that first meeting. Whenever problems pile up on me, I take them to Dr. Peale, and he always comes up with an answer that works for me.

Dr. Peale helped me realize that our professional achievements are secondary; the important thing in life is our relationship with other human beings. It's not what we set out to get, but how we go about the daily task of living.

Dr. Peale advised me to stop feeling guilty. "Is it right for you to worry about your children? You wouldn't have them if God didn't want you to and if He didn't feel you deserved them." He gave me many steadying words to think about when we returned to Hollywood.

That New York trip in the winter of 1954 marked a real turning point in our lives. Before this, we had lived very simply. Whenever the upholstery or the wallpaper needed replacing, I picked the material and patterns as before. Our little ranch house was still a riot of cabbage-rose wallpaper and trailing ivy and petitpoint embroidery.

But we were working so many long hours that the twenty-five-mile commute to the valley was a real problem. So we sold the ranch to Jane Withers and bought a white Georgian brick house next to Jack Benny's on Roxbury Drive in Beverly Hills. Desi also acquired some acres facing the Thunderbird Country Club fairway in Palm Springs, with an uninterrupted view of dazzling green turf and snowcapped Mount San Jacinto. There we built a low, one-story contemporary beige stone house with six bedrooms and six baths, a swimming pool, gardens, and tropical plantings both indoors and out.

We soon found out that although it was one of the most beautiful golf courses in Palm Springs, Thunderbird was also one of the most prejudiced. Not only did it refuse to admit Jews, but, celebrity and property owner or not, Desi was not invited to join either. So Desi, always a frustrated architect at heart, also began building a lavish motel in Palm Springs next to the Indian Wells Country Club. "We won't discriminate against Gentiles, Jews, or Cubans," Desi airily told the press.

Desi sank a million dollars into our Western Hills Motel. It has only forty-two lavish bedrooms, which works out to an investment of about $24,000 per rental unit. The main dining room has a sunken bar which features drinks from Desi's personal Cuban recipes. The architect tested the drinks first and decided to make the bar sunken so customers wouldn't have so far to fall. The house orchestra for a long time was the band Desi toured the country with from 1945 to 1950.

Even though I knew it made sense, it upset me terribly to leave the ranch. I refused to go near the place while everything was being packed. Most of the furniture we gave away, although I still have a few Victorian chairs and beds in my guesthouse in Beverly Hills. I ordered new contemporary living room and bedroom suites from—where else?—Jamestown, New York. The order was flown to Los Angeles in a special chartered airplane.

For the front hallway, I chose a beautiful Japanese silk print that cost ninety dollars a roll—a hideous extravagance,

I thought, but Desi kept assuring me that we could afford it. As soon as it was hung, I realized something I hadn't noticed before—it had shadowy birds all over it. The wallpaper came down the next day.

We spent six months remodeling the Beverly Hills place before we moved in. Finally we had five bedrooms and five baths.

We lived at the Beverly Hills Hotel while the work was being done, and Desi drove himself mercilessly. For years Hollywood had regarded him as just another "hotcha Latin charm boy." They never thought he had the brains or savvy to become a big business tycoon. As a matter of fact, his business acumen amazed me, too. As writer-producer Cy Howard says, "Desi built a television image with tremendous theatrical flair and courage. He was also the shrewdest businessman I ever knew. Unlike most Hollywood tycoons, he could make million-dollar decisions without welshing and without fear."

Desi was by nature an easygoing, music-loving Latin who, left to his own devices, would sleep every day until noon. He learned to be tough but he didn't really enjoy it. Since Desilu was his baby, he felt he had to be on top of every deal. His eighteen-hour days were filled with big business squabbles, clashing personalities, and long hours of rehearsals. Business meetings went on far into the night, and he was generally up and on the telephone with New York by six or seven a.m.

When enough aggravation accumulated, he'd blow his stack at home. At Desilu, he was the kindest, most considerate boss who ever lived. He agreed with me that creative people should be given a lot of leeway and shouldn't have to account for every minute of their time. If a talented writer seldom showed up before two in the afternoon, that was all right with Desi, providing he got his scripts done. But at home, one button off a shirt could make Desi go to pieces.

Finally, on May 5, 1955, our new home was ready for us. Little Lucie and Desi looked forward with glee to all their new playmates in the neighborhood: Dean Martin's seven kids, Jeanne Crain Brinkman's six, and five little Ferrers at Rosemary Clooney's.

Desi carried me over the threshold of our new home with a flourish—then stopped and gasped. During the night, the water pipes in the eighteen-year-old house had burst. The thick white wall-to-wall carpet was a stained, sodden mess; the wallpaper was streaked, the newly plastered walls were disintegrating. Desi really flipped. As the children huddled against me in terror, he ranted, raged, stormed, kicked the walls, and then began tearing them down with his bare hands. "Come, dears," DeDe told the babies, "your father is rehearsing," and she bundled them out of the place.

I had never seen Desi in such a state. I was terrified he was going to seriously hurt himself. I realized for the first time how the strain of our snowballing empire was eating away at him.

A month or two later we finished our fourth season of *I Love Lucy* and immediately began making a movie together, *Forever Darling.*

I haven't been in many flops in my life, but this one

was pretty bad. Desi played a scientist working on a new insecticide; I was his screwball wife who went along on a field trip to help. The picture was made hastily with a poor script; both critics and public panned it.

But at least it inspired a beautiful song and wonderful homecoming to Jamestown, where the world premiere was held early in February 1956. We arrived during a blinding rainstorm, in a helicopter from Buffalo. As I excitedly pointed out the landmarks to Desi, our little whirlybird slowly circled the town, then landed at the high school football field.

Twenty-five thousand people were waiting on the sidewalks to see us. They shouted enthusiastically in the cold, driving rain: mothers with babies, women in sodden fur coats, young and old. DeDe and I were thunderstruck. It was even more exciting to me than our New York reception two years before. Desi was so touched that he left the limousine and rode on top of the fire truck in the parade. He took his hat off to wave and smile, arriving at the hotel drenched and shivering but with the whole city in the palm of his hand. He was absolutely marvelous for the whole three days and charmed everyone.

The most sentimental occasion for me was the party I'd arranged for my Celoron classmates and our beloved principal, Bernard Drake. They came from hundreds of miles away. Some of them I hadn't seen for twenty years. "Now don't tell me your name . . ." I told them, circling the room. I was eager to make my old classmates feel comfortable. Fame can be a tremendous barrier, one I hoped to break down.

I couldn't remember all their names, but in most cases

I could remember some specific thing about them: "Your mother kept a red bowl on the sideboard," or, "You had a green bicycle." The last person in line was a short, bald, sweet-faced man. He looked up shyly while Pauline Lopus smiled impishly at my side. I kept looking at this stranger, totally mystified. At last Pauline burst out, "That's Vinnie."

Vinnie Myers! My eighth-grade beau! Here I had begged Pauline to make certain he'd be there and I didn't even recognize him! Well, I whooped, then hugged and kissed him; Desi came over and shook his hand and slapped him on the back. "So you're the one I've been jealous of all these years!" It was quite the highlight of the trip.

Desi went with me to see Grandfather's little house in Celoron. The yard was still spacious, ringed with great lilac bushes, but the house had shrunk recognizably. The front staircase now had only fifteen short steps; the living room would barely hold a sofa and two armchairs and a TV set; the kitchen shed had been torn down.

Pauline accompanied us to the old Celoron Amusement Park, now waist-high in weeds, its grand promenade a maze of cracked and broken cement, the Ferris wheel, once the world's largest, long since carted off to California. Even the trolley tracks were gone — my onetime road to Jamestown and freedom, whenever I could scrape together the ten-cent fare.

The festivities wound up with a charity ball. I wore my finest feathers, and my old classmates sang "Celoron Will Shine Tonight" while tears dissolved my mascara.

The next day Marion Strong, my old chum and for-

mer New York roommate, asked me to dinner. Amid the am-
brosial smell of freshly baked Swedish rye bread, we dined two
feet from scores of noses and eyes pressed against the win-
dowpanes. The next morning Marion's front lawn looked as
if Ringling Brothers had tarried there. The kid from the
Celoron whistle-stop had "arrived" in Jamestown. What an
emotional wallop that packed.

♥

As we began the 1956–1957 season, the *I Love Lucy*
show still on the top of the heap, we were faced with a
headachy decision: to retire or not to retire. Originally we had
planned a five-year stint with television, and all our contracts
had been written with this deadline in mind. Then we had
planned to quit, take the kids, and sail leisurely around the
world.

But like most idyllic dreams, this one didn't seem too
practical on closer inspection. It was tremendously exciting
building a new company; from seven employees we had grown
to one thousand, and not one of them had resigned in Desilu's
five years of existence. It was a young organization—our employees' average age was thirty-two—and a sense of family was
always emphasized, between company picnics, bowling con-
tests, trips to Disneyland, and New Year's Eve parties at the
ranch, where Desi presided like a grand *patrón*.

Besides *I Love Lucy*, we owned six other shows on television. Filming took place on our lot for the *Wyatt Earp* and
Danny Thomas shows, *December Bride*, the Eve Arden and Red

Skelton shows, and *The Real McCoys*. Often, during the busy season, we had two thousand people on our payroll. Could we turn our backs on them and sail away?

And how do you quit a number-one show? I wasn't ready to sit gazing at Mount San Jacinto. And Desi didn't seem to enjoy the same kind of leisure activities anymore. A few years ago, he'd look forward to spending his weekends happily puttering around the ranch. Evenings we'd have friends in for dinner and charades. I *still* preferred to spend my weekends resting, playing cards, and sitting on the floor with the kids. But now, by the weekend, Desi was too keyed up and restless for such simple pleasures. After we finished filming the show Friday nights, a limousine and station wagon transported the sleeping children, Desi's mother, and Desi and me to our home at Del Mar or Palm Springs. Desi would make sure that we were all comfortably at home, and then he'd disappear. It was go, go, go all the time: to the golf links, to his new motel, the gambling tables, or his yacht.

He stopped discussing any of our personal problems. I had to dig and dig to discover what caused his rages, and generally it had nothing to do with anything I'd done. I wanted to help him, find out where I was at fault. But as soon as I started questioning, he'd stalk angrily out of the room. Or the house.

On the set, my attention to detail began to annoy him. He was spending six hours at his desk for every two hours in rehearsals, and there were constant interruptions with phone calls and meetings.

Finally, we decided to stay on as president and vice

president of Desilu but to cut down the work schedule. In the spring of 1957, we finished the last of the half-hour *I Love Lucy* shows and signed a $12 million contract with Westinghouse for a series of monthly one-hour comedy specials, starting in the fall. (The following year, we would negotiate the sale of the 179 *I Love Lucy* shows back to CBS for more than $5 million, another significant addition to our working capital.)

In September 1957, I flew to New York to talk to Dr. Norman Vincent Peale. He steered me to the codirector of his American Foundation of Religion and Psychiatry, the well-known psychiatrist Dr. Smiley Blanton, the author of *Love or Perish*.

Dr. Blanton was a frail, slight man who spoke in a penetrating whisper. For most of September I saw him two or three hours a day. We kept trying to get Desi to see Dr. Blanton too, but with no luck. Finally, in October, Desi gave in to my entreaties and flew to New York. Dr. Blanton came to our suite at the Hampshire House at nine one morning and remained with us until six in the evening.

I was grateful that Desi was finally facing some of our personal issues. It was like old times at the ranch, both of us pacing up and down the hotel room yelling at the top of our voices, then doubling over with laughter, and kicking chair legs and throwing pillows. The discussion was simply great; we both felt so much better by dinnertime. We left the apartment arm in arm and went on to have a perfectly marvelous evening, while Dr. Blanton went home to have a good, long rest.

Desi saw Dr. Blanton a few times after that, but he never really warmed to analysis and he refused to admit that he had any problem. He went back to Hollywood while I stayed in New York another month for sessions with Dr. Blanton. Cleo moved into the Hampshire House with me and we stuck close to our suite most of the time, venturing out only to see all the new Broadway shows.

A month later I was back at work on the new hour-long Lucy-Desi comedy specials. One day in late November, Desi was detained at his office for an unusually long time. Finally he phoned down to tell me why. I hung up and told the director and the cast, "Desi will be late." I added, "He's buying RKO."

I learned that Dan O'Shea of RKO had phoned to ask Desi if he wanted to buy all their properties for $6,500,000. Desi had never even considered such a thing, but we badly needed more space.

That night, November 27, 1957, between the second and third acts of our show, we closed the deal for $6,150,000. The next day, Desi toured the RKO studios like a kid discovering Disneyland. We now owned thirty-three more soundstages, or eleven more than 20th Century–Fox and four more than MGM. We had fabulous permanent sets, including the Southern plantation, Tara, from *Gone With the Wind*, fire-scarred and weather-beaten but still majestic. In the wardrobe department were gowns once worn by Carole Lombard, Irene Dunne, and Katharine Hepburn, and even a few of mine from *Roberta* and *Big Street*. Desi found an entire warehouse full of wallpaper. "No more paper at ninety dollars a roll!" he told me jubilantly. But when he came home that night and learned that I had just ordered a new white grand piano for the living room, he flipped. "We've got nineteen grand pianos at RKO!"

In January 1958, we signed the final escrow papers. As I signed away $6,150,000, my hand shook. But in our business, money becomes an exchange of legal documents; I never saw much real cash and never really *felt* rich either.

Despite the big transaction, we stuck to our decision about cutting back on work. Now, for the first time in five years, I had two free weeks every month, even during the busy season, and three months free every summer. Finally I had time to attend to matters I'd long neglected. With the help of a professional cutter from the studio, I tackled our twenty-eight thousand feet of home color movies. After four weeks of hard work, we had thirty consecutive hours of film, from the babies' first hour and first step and tooth through every family birthday and holiday. Next I tore through the house weeding out closets, until the household staff was in a frenzy.

In the fall of 1958, I was invited to address a class in Hollywood on comedy techniques; I went once and then was invited back for twenty-two weeks.

That summer, I damn near went crazy. I had too much on my mind and too much time on my hands. I started redecorating the whole studio, changed the color schemes in all the ladies' rooms, and repainted the reception building . . . *twice!* I had to put all this restless energy to *some* good use. That's when I remembered how much I had enjoyed my teaching experience and decided to reactivate Lela Rogers's theater work-shop on the RKO lot. Her original theater was still standing, although it cost $90,000 to put it back into shape. My idea was to give some talented youngsters a boost into show business. I wanted to get a group who would work well together. This took me five weeks, auditioning eight hours a day. I finally chose twenty-one kids, of whom five didn't work out. Most of the group were in their twenties. All talented, eager, and tire-less. Eventually, nine of our original sixteen landed television and movie contracts. I found out you have to be a lay analyst to direct, however. Inevitably you get all involved in their per-sonal lives. Carole Cook, for example, a dynamite musical comedy talent, lived in our home for a while and I was matron of honor at her wedding. Running the workshop became a round-the-clock job, but I found that rehearsing ten and twelve hours a day was a constructive way to take my mind off my troubles. Fortunately, Desi was busy too, so we were able to pretty much stay out of each other's way.

At that time, Desi was the studio's top salesman, chief executive officer, and programming director. He had just con-cluded our company's most successful year with a $24 million gross business and net profits over $800,000. Things had never been better for Desilu. We wished we could say the same for Desi and Lucy.

In November 1958, the Hollywood Friars' Club hon-ored Desi and me with a hilarious roasting. Harry Einstein, oth-erwise known as Parkyakarkas, had just finished a screaming monologue when he was stricken with a heart attack. Art Linkletter asked if there was a doctor in the audience, and five heart specialists rushed up. In a back room they fought for two hours to save Harry's life, but failed. Desi, upon acknowledging the Friars' honor, said, "This meant so much to me. Now it means nothing. They say the show must go on. Why must it?"

The following spring, I made my last effort toward a reconciliation with Desi. We took the children, then seven and six; their nanny; Cleo and her husband, Kenny Morgan; Harriet; and forty-eight pieces of luggage to Europe: Paris, Rome, Capri, and London.

In England I had my first experience with the British press. *I Love Lucy* was one of the top shows in the British Isles, and we had warm demonstrations from fans wherever we went. But that press conference was something else again: "How much money do you have?" "How old are you? . . . Really? Well, if you admit to that, you must be five years older." Unbelievable. I just looked at them. I turned from one to the other with a cold, impassive stare. Then some woman grabbed little Lucie and took her behind a potted palm. "What's it like to be rich?" she asked. "Is it true your father and mother fight all the time?" I went behind the palm and took Lucie's hand. *"If* you don't mind," I told that monstrous woman of the tabloid press. On the other side of the room were five perfect ladies and gentlemen from the London *Times* and the Manchester *Guardian.* "May I see all of you tomorrow?" I asked them. They said yes, of course, and left, terribly embarrassed for their colleagues.

Big Desi was restless, uncommunicative, and bored.

When he wasn't drinking, he spent most of his time on the phone with the studio or checking the Del Mar racetrack, where his horses were running. I was completely disenchanted, bitter, and unforgiving . . . and the kids saw and heard way too much.

Desi and I came back from our trip not speaking. He moved into the guesthouse and then went abroad again, alone this time, for several months.

I realized we never really liked each other. We had a great attraction going for each other in the beginning but we didn't approve of each other. He disapproved of my moderation and my conservatism. I was square, he said. I disapproved of the way he worked too hard, played too hard, and was never moderate in anything. It was like living on top of a volcano; you never knew when it would erupt or why.

I was able to accept the situation for many years because it was our secret. Anonymity is a great thing when you're unhappy. But when Desi made it public domain, I knew I couldn't be publicly embarrassed any longer. My only to-die moments in life have been when I've lost my self-respect. And Desi's conduct toward me in front of other people became more and more humiliating.

I'm all activity on the outside, but I have fewer inner anxieties than Desi. I have my grandparents and DeDe to thank for that. I'm a strong, independent woman, but making myself weaker didn't help Desi. I had to realize that deep down he wanted to make all the mistakes in the book and wanted to suffer the consequences. He needed to punish himself. Toward the end of our marriage, he was practically jumping out windows.

I was at fault too. I had lost my good humor and sense of proportion. When you're too mad and too rattled to see straight, you're bound to make mistakes. You can't go on and on for years being miserable about a situation and not have it change you. You get so you can't stand yourself.

I decided to divorce Desi.

During this period, Vivian Vance was getting her divorce from Phil Ober, and she was upset and miserable, too.

Vivian and I have always been extraordinarily compatible, so we were especially close during this time of misery. Occasionally, however, our tempers grew short; this was a very rough spell for all of us.

One day Vivian and I had a disagreement on the set and stopped speaking. The silence went on much longer than either of us anticipated. It got to be a nuisance, since we were so used to listening carefully to each other's lines and making suggestions. But this particular Thursday we spent in stony silence.

Finally it was only an hour before the actual performance. We usually spent this time buoying each other up to get into the proper relaxed and joyous mood for performing. We sat side by side, putting on our makeup. Although not a word had been spoken, I suddenly blurted out, "Vivian, you know that line"—I repeated it—"you're not reading it right. It should be . . ." And I gave her my interpretation.

"Gee," she replied, "you're right. Why didn't you say so before?"

"Well," I replied heatedly, "we weren't speaking, and I'd be damned if I'd tell you!"

Our eyes met in the mirror and we collapsed into laughter. We could never stay cross with each other for very long.

By the spring of 1960, Desi and I were totally estranged, although he still had to be both actor and director on the show. The good-natured kidding that used to animate the set disappeared entirely. The fun was gone. It saddened Vivian and Bill and our entire crew to watch the painful disintegration of what had been our Camelot. I remember Irma Kusely, our hairdresser, saying, "We all knew it was over. It was so sad. There was nothing anyone could do." Finally I stopped speaking to Desi altogether. "Lucy dear," he'd say with elaborate politeness, "would you please step over here when you say that line?" and I'd follow his directions without a word.

In one of our last shows I played a geisha girl. My face was covered with white powder. My eyes were red from hours of weeping. Whenever I looked at Desi, I could feel my expression hardening. Cold, implacable hate oozed through every pore, for Desi, and for myself too. I loathed my new self, but I couldn't bring myself to ask Desi for a divorce. He had to be the one to make the break.

Soon after this episode was shot, Desi asked me for a divorce. I had a lawyer in his office in twenty minutes. The day I filed for the divorce, on grounds of "extreme mental cruelty"—March 3, 1960—we were filming an hour show with Ernie Kovacs and his wife, Edie Adams. In the episode, Lucy tries to get Ricky on Ernie's TV show. To disguise myself, I wore a chauffeur's uniform with cap and mustache. In the final scene, Desi was supposed to pull me into an embrace, mustache and all, and kiss me.

When the scene arrived and the cameras closed in for that final embrace, we just looked at each other, and then Desi kissed me, and we both cried. It marked the end of so many things.

♥

I wasn't in great shape physically, having suffered two bouts of pneumonia that year, but now I threw myself into work with a vengeance. I planned to do a movie with Bob Hope that summer called *The Facts of Life,* then a Broadway musical, *Wildcat.* I had considered doing a play based on Dorothy Parker's *Big Blonde,* but decided it had too much pathos for my depressed state of mind. I wanted something joyful and upbeat. The role of Wildcat Jackson, "the cat with more bounce to the ounce," seemed right.

After that, the children and I would live in Switzerland, I decided. I would sell both the Beverly Hills and Palm Springs places and make my permanent base in Europe amid all that lovely white snow and clear mountain air. I wanted to get as far away from Hollywood and Desi as humanly possible. He could run Desilu and I would remove myself permanently. It didn't work out that way, but that was my original idea.

*Lucille with
second husband, Gary Morton,
to whom she was married
from 1961 until
her death in 1989.*

Chapter 14

♥

When unhappiness piles up, work has always been my salvation. I threw myself into my next few projects, eager to lose myself in work. It helped me mentally, but physically I wound up worse off.

In *The Facts of Life,* my first film project after the breakup, Bob Hope and I had a hilarious script and inspired direction from Mel Frank and Norman Panama. We played a couple of old family friends who find themselves accidentally thrown together on a vacation and fall helplessly in love. The comic aspects develop when their romance soars melodiously, only to hit a succession of sour notes. Dumping the old spouse for a new one turns out to be more trouble than it's worth.

We were filming the movie at Desilu, and using the same Stage 12 where I was used to doing *I Love Lucy*. Everything went along merrily until we came to the scene where Bob and Kitty, out fishing, realize they're falling in love. Kitty catches her first fish. In her excitement, she turns to Bob and throws her arms around his neck. During this scene we had the six-foot tank underneath the stage filled with water and a real boat floating on it, tied to a fake pier.

Bob and I did the scene and then the director, Mel Frank, decided he wanted an extra little look of trepidation between us after our first kiss. To get this, the cameras and lights had to be rearranged, so Bob and I stepped off the boat.

Bob went over to sit with the director a moment, and Mel remarked, "It's amazing that with all this physical stuff, nobody's even scratched a finger." Famous last words.

At that point, an assistant came forward to help me into the boat again. In a spurt of good spirits, I shrugged him away and took one little leap. My foot caught on the side of the boat and I fell headlong into it, landing on my left temple.

By the time the ambulance came, I had a lump over my left eye the size of a goose egg. My right leg burned like fury where the side of the boat had torn a big flap off my shin, but it was my head injury which concerned everyone most.

Desi was notified about the accident while at his horse ranch. He raced the forty miles to Cedars of Lebanon Hospital. When he learned that all I had was a bad concussion, he wired Bob: "I played straight man to her for nine years and never pushed her. Why couldn't you control yourself?"

L O V E ,   L U C Y

By the middle of July, after several weeks of convalescence, I was back on the set.

A few days after we finished *The Facts of Life*, I flew to New York to begin a new career. The ambition of my life was going to be realized at last: my name in lights on Broadway. *Wildcat*, by N. Richard Nash, author of *The Rainmaker*, had originally been written as a drama. By the time we started rehearsals in August, it was a musical with some really great songs by Cy Coleman and Carolyn Leigh.

How I was going to sing them, I had no idea. I'd never been a singer, not even in the bathtub. I'd never been a dancer, either, and *Wildcat* had me just about climbing walls.

The play was set in a western town in 1912. Wildcat Jackson swings into town, a broke but beguiling female in dungarees determined to strike oil. She teaches her crippled sister, Janie, that a bold face to misfortune will always turn the trick. Wildy was tough, calculating, rough-talking, and unbelievably energetic. By the time I had mastered all her calisthenics, my thigh muscles were like cords of steel.

After a week of rehearsals with my leading man, Keith Andes, and Paula Stewart, who played my lame sister, a bright red spot appeared on my shin where I had fallen during the filming of *The Facts of Life*. The cut had healed over completely, but an infection had started near the bone. I checked into the Polyclinic Hospital on West Fiftieth Street, where a surgeon opened up the wound and scraped away nylon stocking from the inside.

With my bandaged leg resting on a pillow, I spent

hours practicing the songs I would be singing in *Wildcat*. Friends stopping by to commiserate found a very merry Lucy. They couldn't shut me up. I just kept singing. One song in particular I embraced more than any other: "Hey, Look Me Over!"—the one I grew to love at the hospital—eventually became *my* song. Thereafter, if there was an orchestra around when I entered some room, they'd start playing it. I was glad to be identified with such an upbeat tune.

During the weeks I was spending in rehearsal, the children were with their father at the beach and the ranch. In the fall, DeDe; Harriet; the children; their nanny, Willie Mae Barker; and our chauffeur, Frank Gorey, all joined me in the vast apartment I'd rented on the sixteenth floor of the Imperial House with a thirty-eight-foot terrace. I naively thought the kids could play outdoors on the terrace, high above the Lexington Avenue traffic. I kept thinking how great it would be for them to enjoy a change of seasons—autumn leaves, snow, spring flowers. But they took an instant dislike to New York's gray November skies and chill. DeDe accompanied them back and forth to the neighborhood parochial school.

Everywhere the kids went, a big fuss was made over them. They missed their father and their friends in California, but both of them were really good sports about the move, although they did miss, too, the freedom of playing outdoors wherever they wanted.

After two strenuous months of rehearsals, *Wildcat* opened in Philadelphia on October 30, 1960. Desi flew in from Hollywood and was full of suggestions about how the show could be improved. He even brought my two writers, Bob and Madelyn, from the West Coast to help, but because of a union rule, they couldn't add so much as a comma to the script.

This role was the most physically strenuous of my career. After a month of playing *Wildcat,* I had shed nineteen pounds and was covered with black-and-blue marks. I'd broken two fingers, sprained my ankle three times, and had my left leg bandaged under my tight blue jeans to support a pulled tendon. But I felt on top of the world.

The play stayed in Philadelphia for two months, with mild notices from the critics but playing to packed houses for the duration. DeDe and the children came down from New York every weekend; we couldn't keep little Lucie *out* of the theater. She saw *Wildcat* seventeen times!

The big New York opening came December 15. Planeloads of friends arrived and surged up to my apartment that afternoon; I guess it was one of the biggest thrills in my life. "Why don't you lie down and rest?" Cleo kept urging me, but I was much too excited. Instead, I washed and set Lucie's hair for the opening.

We opened in a driving New York blizzard. A theater full of "worshipful admirers," as the press put it, seemed to enjoy themselves hugely. Afterward, Desi threw a big party at "21" in my honor, and we sat waiting for the reviews to appear. As the party wore on, the gaiety seemed to me to wear thin.

Finally I went over to Cleo and whispered, "Let's leave . . . I know they're keeping the reviews from me." On our way back to the apartment, we stopped to pick up four or five papers. They were full of "Welcome, Lucy" stuff but were tepid about the show. I had hoped for a big fat hit, at least for the sake of our wonderful cast. I was deeply disappointed.

About a week after our opening, Paula Stewart suggested a midnight supper with her fella, comedian Jack Carter, at their favorite pizza place.

"We've got a friend we'd like you to meet," Paula said, "Gary Morton. You'll like him—he's a great guy."

My first reaction was to say no. I was usually exhausted after a performance. I had underestimated what it took to give life to my character eight times a week.

But Paula persuaded me to go along, so I joined them later at the restaurant. Gary says the thing he liked first about me was the way I walked, head up, like a thoroughbred. But as soon as I reached the table, I just about collapsed, and started griping about how tired I was.

"Light me a cigarette," I said offhandedly to this big, tanned six-footer. I tossed a cigarette in his direction.

Gary picked it up and tossed it right back. "Here," he said, "light it yourself."

I started laughing. Before long, I was jabbing him in those broad shoulders of his and saying, "Who are you? What do you do?"

Gary jabbed me right back. "I'm a nightclub performer. What's your line?"

I didn't know it at the time, but Gary had never seen me on television. During the nine years we'd been on, he had

never caught a single *I Love Lucy* show. He says this was because he was usually backstage at some theater or supper club
getting ready for a nine-o'clock performance.

When I met him in 1960, Gary had been a popular
stand-up comedian for fifteen years in this country and in
England and Australia. He'd started doing imitations while in
the Army in Fort Riley, Kansas. He told his family he wanted
to be a variety entertainer and, "If I don't make the Paramount
in five years, I'll quit." He made it in three. He had toured with
Johnny Ray for a year and had been an understudy for the
Broadway run of *Mr. Wonderful.* He had also been on bills with
Dean Martin, Frank Sinatra, Sammy Davis, Milton Berle,
Lena Horne, and many others. More than a stand-up, Gary
was a monologuist with a built-in sense of humor and a flair
for zeroing in on the absurdities of life. He didn't need a putty
nose or baggy pants to be howlingly funny.

I realized Gary had the natural humor of someone
who loves to laugh and wants everyone to laugh with him. That
made two of us.

When that first evening ended and Gary took me
home, I felt more like myself than I had in months.

I met Gary on December 20. The next day he left for
Ohio for a series of nightclub engagements that would keep
him away from New York and his friends and family until after
New Year's. I was amazed at the complacency with which he
accepted this exile for the holidays.

I sensed in him a great loneliness and a hunger for a
family, but at the same time, a wonderful, philosophic calm.

There is an acceptance and balance about him. And unlike so many of us in show business, he isn't plagued by dozens of insecurities. He gives his best and seems naturally resistant to the kind of doubt that eats away at so many other performers.

I guess it didn't take Gary long to realize that beneath my rather brassy exterior, I'm very soft and dependent.

When he got back to New York, he asked if he could call for me every evening after the show. Soon after this he asked me, "Will you be my girl?" We were sitting at a table with six or so other people and I was so startled I didn't know what to say. Finally I said I'd have to think it over, but I didn't go out with anyone else after that.

In February, I came down with a bad virus and flew to Miami for some sunshine. Because of my leg, which was still giving me a bad time, the doctors kept pumping me full of antibiotics.

After a couple of weeks, we opened the show again, but the virus persisted. During the last week in April, I fainted onstage during a song-and-dance routine. A month later, I fainted again. By this time they were giving me oxygen backstage to keep me going. Both DeDe and Gary were urging me to quit. "Lucille! The Man upstairs is trying to tell you something!" DeDe told me. But I ignored her warning.

Since I'd backed the show, I didn't have to worry about friends or unknown angels losing money in the production, which had been a sellout from the beginning. But I worried about my supporting players and the gypsies, the dancers and singers who migrate from show to show. I wanted them all to have the run of the show, which, in spite of the reviews, promised to be a long one.

Ultimately, I just couldn't keep it up, much as I'd wanted to. One night in May, seven months after we had opened in Philadelphia, I collapsed onstage and my doctors ordered me to close the show. We turned back $165,000 at the box office, but my pride suffered more than my pocketbook. When my energy wanes, it embarrasses me terribly. I hate being sick or incapacitated in any way. Hedda Hopper wrote, "Let's hope Lucy stays in the hospital until she regains her health, strength and peace of mind. Lucy's one of the most vital girls I know but so weak now she can scarcely hold a teacup."

I felt so awful I honestly thought I was going to die. So instead of checking into a hospital, I flew to London and eventually to Capri and Rome, determined to die in a scenic atmosphere.

I felt deeply depressed about having closed the show, but eventually I recovered my spirits before my health.

After I returned from my trip abroad, I crawled back to Beverly Hills. I never did get to enjoy much of my beautiful New York apartment. Gary soon followed me out west. He stayed in our guesthouse for several weeks. For the first time we saw him under normal, everyday circumstances, away from the theater and nightclubs.

When we went to Hollywood parties, Gary says, he felt like "some strange lamp." Everyone circled around, looking at him from every angle. But I soon discovered that he had more friends in show business than I did.

During that summer I was convalescing, Gary kept bringing up the subject of marriage and I kept hedging. I seriously questioned whether I could make any man happy. I worried about the slight difference in our ages and the effect my career might have on him.

Finally DeDe said, "Why don't you get married? You shouldn't let that guy get away."

I asked the children how they felt about my getting married again.

"Will Daddy like it?" they asked.

"He wouldn't mind," I told them.

I've always wanted to share with someone the good and the bad. Especially when things are *good*, you need someone. Some people should never marry, because they don't know how to share and have no desire to. Gary had been traveling for fifteen years, in and out of cities constantly. With that kind of life, it's almost impossible to sustain any serious relationship when you're away so much. He had been married once, very briefly, and it had been annulled in 1957. By this time, he was forty-six and ready and anxious for a family — something money can't buy.

When I divorced Desi I had no intention of ever marrying again, but this guy did seem too good to let get away. Years ago, I picked up a little book called *The Art of Selfishness*. This little book revolutionized my life. It taught me to worry less about all the outside factors in my life and take command of *me*. I learned to subject everything in my life to these questions: "Is this *good* for *Lucy*? Does it fill my needs? Is it good for my health, my peace of mind? Does my conscience agree, does it give me a spiritual lift?" No wonder I had been feeling so happy and secure. The answer was simple: Gary was good for Lucy.

So, after I'd known Gary for eleven months, I decided to take the big step. We were on a plane flying to New York, where Gary had a date at the Copa and I was going to do a TV show with Henry Fonda. Gary proposed again.

"Lucy, what are we waiting for?"

"Well," I hedged, "are you prepared for any swipes that they might take at you? What if they call you Mr. Ball?"

Gary answered quietly, "Who are *they?*"

"All right," I said. "If Dr. Norman Vincent Peale is free to marry us this week, we'll go ahead."

From that moment on, I had no qualms, no apprehension. We liked each other before we loved each other. We approve of each other; neither of us is trying to change the other. Gary has a maturity I admire.

Before our marriage, Gary spoke with my lawyers without my knowledge and offered to sign away any interest in my money. He has always made an excellent living, and we keep our bank accounts separate.

Dr. Peale was free to marry us in his Marble Collegiate Church on November 19, 1961. The whole thing was quickly arranged, in only five days. The children flew east with DeDe to be part of our new lives from the beginning. We purposely had a small, intimate wedding with as much dignity and love as we could put into it, instead of flying off somewhere into the hinterlands for a few hurried words by a justice of the peace.

We invited only forty people to the church service and barred all press and television cameras except my adored Hedda Hopper. During the fifteen-minute service, the organ softly played "Make Someone Happy," a song that had become a favorite of ours early in our courtship. When Dr. Peale pronounced us man and wife, the wedding guests applauded!

Gary smiled and kissed me.

"There may be a few Lucy fans waiting outside," we were warned as we prepared to leave. There had been perhaps fifty waiting on the sidewalk when we arrived.

We were dumbfounded when we left the church to find a thousand people jamming the Fifth Avenue sidewalk! They were smiling and calling out, "Good luck, Lucy," and, "We're with you, Lucy." It made us feel very, very good—starting our life together with so many good wishes.

In 1957 RKO became Desilu Studios. In 1962 Lucille bought Desi's controlling interest in the company, thus becoming the first woman president of a major television studio.

C h a p t e r
1 5
♥

*G*ary and I honeymooned right in Beverly Hills with the children. For five months I sat and did nothing. For the first time in my life I learned how to relax. But by March, Desi had talked me into doing a new television series without him or Bill Frawley. By then, Bill had joined Fred MacMurray in the highly popular show *My Three Sons*. And Desi had discovered a book by Irene Kampen called *Life Without George*, about two women trying to raise their children without husbands, which he thought could be a great basis for a new series for me.

I refused even to consider being in a continuing series without Vivian. Since we had gone off the air, she had married a handsome and successful New York literary agent, John Dodds. They had bought a century-old house in Stamford, Connecticut, and Vivian was ecstatic about her flower garden, singing in the local church choir, and lecturing on behalf of mental health. Her loyalty to me — and a hefty paycheck — won her back to my side.

Vivian has always been the greatest supporting player anyone could ask for. During one of the shows in this new series, we were supposed to be trapped in a glass shower stall, with the water turned on full blast. The script called for me to dive down and pull out the plug at the bottom of the shower, but when I did this in front of a live audience, I found I had no room to maneuver. I couldn't get back to the surface again. What's more, I had swallowed a lot of water, and was actually drowning, right there in front of three hundred people who were splitting their sides laughing.

Vivian, realizing in cold terror what had happened, never changed expression. She reached down, pulled me safely to the surface by the roots of my hair, and then calmly spoke both sides of our dialogue, putting my lines in the form of questions. Whatta girl! And whatta night! When I finally had the strength to climb out of the shower stall and, as usual, reach for the mike to say good night to the audience, I suddenly heard Gary's voice from the sidelines: "Don't touch that mike!" I froze, dripping wet, an inch from that live microphone. Gary had saved me from potential electrocution!

During this time, Desi was still head of Desilu and executive producer of our new *Lucy Show,* but having both Desi and Gary on the set at the same time proved to be too much. Desi was getting anxious to retire, anyway. Eleven years at the helm of Desilu had taken its toll and he was ready to devote more time to his horses and his golf.

At first I thought that we should bring someone else in to run Desilu, but it didn't prove to be that simple. So in November 1962, I bought Desi out to the tune of $3 million and he retired. The board of directors then persuaded me to be president, and I reluctantly agreed.

*I've become a woman
with a capacity for
happiness again."*

_C h a p t e r_
_1 6_
♥

As December of 1962 approached, I yearned to spend a real old-fashioned white Christmas with Gary and the children. Gary loathed cold weather and thrived on sunshine. He also spent so many Christmas holidays on the road that all he wanted to do at this time of year was stay home.

But I had the children to consider. Desi had them for all the summer holidays; they were with me during the school year. I was the one who had to keep after them about their homework and music lessons. So I always tried to plan some special fun for them at Christmas and Easter.

At first I tried to persuade the family to fly to Switzerland for Christmas, but they thought New England was far away enough. So I phoned Bette Davis and said, "If anybody knows New England, *you* do. Where shall we go for Christmas?" She suggested two places and we chose Franconia, New Hampshire. We made arrangements to stay in a small chalet.

When I travel, I leave very little at home. If the children aren't with me, I take several of their pictures off the wall to bring along. When they were small, I used to fly their sleds to Sun Valley with us, plus their Samoyed, Blanquito, to pull them uphill. Since the kids were coming along, I didn't need to pack the photos, but I made sure to bring all the necessary pots and pans; boxes of groceries and favorite food; ice skates and ski equipment; and of course, tree ornaments as well as everyone's Christmas gifts.

One thing we learned at Franconia was that we were used to lots of living space. At the chalet, the four of us crowded into one tiny cottage with bunk beds under the rafters and one bathroom. The luggage and seven-foot Christmas tree barely left us room to squeeze into our beds. We soon gave up cooking and went out for every meal; this meant bundling up and mushing through the snow and cold. "And to think we have that wonderful place in Palm Springs," Gary moaned, blowing on the twenty-seventh fire that refused to burn.

The skating pond was a flooded tennis court so bumpy that little Lucie said, "They must have frozen the tennis balls in it." The ski slopes seemed very narrow and cramped after Sun Valley, where every skier could use the lift and get off wherever he wanted. At Franconia, only the experienced skiers were allowed to use the lift; this relegated us to the lower slopes.

We had planned to stay for two weeks, but after about four days we mushed out and spent the rest of our vacation time at our beautiful place in Palm Springs.

The next month we followed Gary to a Pebble Beach golf tournament. At the Del Monte Lodge we celebrated little Desi's birthday. Across the room sat big Desi. It had been ten years since little Desi was born. The night of his birthday he played the drums with the lodge orchestra while proud mama and papa clapped from separate tables. And when he blew out the candles on his birthday cake, Desi came over to give him a paternal hug and kiss.

Two months later, at the Sands Hotel in Las Vegas, Desi celebrated his forty-sixth birthday by marrying another redhead, Mrs. Edith Mack Hirsch. I've known Edie for years. She's a sweet woman, and good for Desi. She also shares his great interest in fishing and in horses. Desi seems to be much happier and healthier now in retirement. I'm glad for our children's sake that they now have two happy homes rather than one miserable, unhappy one. Desi and I keep in close touch about the children in a way we never could when we were married.

I'm grateful for the amicable feeling now between Desi and me and Gary and the children. Desi phones me often to discuss the children or the show, and he plays golf with Gary. Since our lives have been straightened out, the children have improved in their schoolwork and they laugh more. Children internalize their parents' unhappiness. Fortunately, they absorb our contentment just as readily.

Gary has wisely not tried to force himself on them or to buy their favor with presents; he hasn't refrained from being the firm disciplinarian, either, when that's indicated. When they hear that deep basso voice of his, they hop to it! And when they want to play, he's available. He swims with them and takes them golfing. He wrestles with them and lets them chase him through the house shrieking with laughter, the sound I like best.

I'm happiest when I'm working, rising to challenges. With Gary, I've become a woman with a capacity for happiness again.

When he first came to visit us in Beverly Hills, before we were married, Gary made the mistake of saying that he had run a movie projector in the Army. Out came my thirty consecutive hours of home movies. Bachelor Gary was too polite to protest; I had him running baby pictures for days. Recently I told him I've got another twenty thousand feet or so, including our family holiday in the chalet at Franconia.

"Geez, Lucy, don't you *ever* go *off* the air?"

Hopefully not.